FIX-IT and FORGET-IT®

PROTEIN-PACKED MEALS

Fix-It and Forget-It® PROTEIN-PACKED MEALS

Slow-Cooker and Instant Pot Recipes to Power Your Day

HOPE COMERFORD

Photos by Bonnie Matthews

New York, New York

Library of Congress Cataloging-in-Publication Data is available on file.

Cover design by Kai Texel
Cover image credit: Bonnie Matthews

Print ISBN: 978-1-964219-19-6
Ebook ISBN: 978-1-964219-38-7

Printed in China

Contents

Welcome to *Fix-It and Forget-It Protein-Packed Meals!*

You're not alone if you've ever finished a meal and still felt hungry an hour later, or if you've struggled to find the balance between healthy and feeling satisfied. One of the biggest reasons people turn to higher-protein food options is because they feel full, fueled, and energized after eating instead of hungry, empty, and tired!

Fix-It and Forget-It Protein-Packed Meals contains recipes to help support your body and give you the energy you need to take on your day. It can be challenging to get enough protein in your diet daily, but let this book help you do it in a way that is fun and flavorful! A high-protein diet doesn't have to be boring. From creative breakfasts that will keep you going all morning, to delicious and satisfying dinners to keep you fueled until bedtime, this book has you covered. Top it all off with a healthy and rewarding guilt-free dessert.

To help further, nutrition info is included for all recipes in this book. Keep in mind, if you alter the ingredients, the nutrition info will no longer be accurate. Do not let that stop you from making necessary changes to accommodate your dietary and/or food restrictions. Cooking is always about making the food work for you.

Discover how delicious a high-protein diet can be! Let's get cooking with food that truly fuels and energizes you! Enjoy!

Choosing a Slow Cooker

Not all slow cookers are created equal . . . or work equally as well for everyone!

Those of us who use slow cookers frequently know we have our own preferences when it comes to which slow cooker we choose to use. For instance, I love my programmable slow cooker, but there are many programmable slow cookers I've tried that I've strongly disliked. Why? Because some go by increments of 15 or 30 minutes and some go by 4, 6, 8, or 10 hours. I dislike those restrictions, but I have family and friends who don't mind them at all! I am also pretty brand loyal when it comes to my manual slow cookers because I've had great success with those and have had unsuccessful moments with slow cookers of other brands. So, which slow cooker(s) is/are best for your household?

It really depends on how many people you're feeding and if you're gone for long periods of time. Here are my recommendations:

For 2–3 person household	3–5 quart slow cooker
For 4–5 person household	5–6 quart slow cooker
For 6+ person household	6½–7 quart slow cooker

Large Slow Cooker Advantages/Disadvantages:

Advantages:
- You can fit a loaf pan or a baking dish into a 6- or 7-quart, depending on the shape of your cooker. That allows you to make bread or cakes, or even smaller quantities of main dishes. (Take your favorite baking dish and loaf pan along when you shop for a cooker to make sure they'll fit inside.)
- You can feed large groups of people, or make larger quantities of food, allowing for leftovers, or meals, to freeze.

Disadvantages:
- They take up more storage room.
- They don't fit as neatly into a dishwasher.
- If your crock isn't ⅔–¾ full, you may burn your food.

Small Slow Cooker Advantages/Disadvantages:

Advantages:
- They're great for lots of appetizers, for serving hot drinks, for baking cakes straight in the crock, and for dorm rooms or apartments.
- Great option for making recipes of smaller quantities.

Disadvantages:
- Food in smaller quantities tends to cook more quickly than larger amounts. So keep an eye on it.
- Chances are, you won't have many leftovers. So, if you like to have leftovers, a smaller slow cooker may not be a good option for you.

My Recommendation:

Have at least two slow cookers; one around 3 to 4 quarts and one 6 quarts or larger. A third would be a huge bonus (and a great advantage to your cooking repertoire!). The advantage of having at least a couple is you can make a larger variety of recipes. Also, you can make at least two or three dishes at once for a whole meal.

Manual vs. Programmable

If you are gone for only six to eight hours a day, a manual slow cooker might be just fine for you. If you are gone for more than eight hours during the day, I would highly recommend purchasing a programmable slow cooker that will switch to warm when the cook time you set is up. It will allow you to cook a wider variety of recipes.

The two I use most frequently are my 4-quart manual slow cooker and my 6½-quart programmable slow cooker. I like that I can make smaller portions in my 4-quart slow cooker on days I don't need or want leftovers, but I also love how my 6½-quart slow cooker can accommodate whole chickens, turkey breasts, hams, or big batches of soups. I use them both often.

Get to Know Your Slow Cooker . . .

Plan a little time to get acquainted with your slow cooker. Each slow cooker has its own personality—just like your oven (and your car). Plus, many new slow cookers cook hotter and faster than earlier models. I think that with all of the concern for food safety, the slow cooker manufacturers have amped up their settings so that High, Low, and Warm are all higher temperatures than in the older models. That means they cook hotter—and therefore, faster— than the first slow cookers. The beauty of these little machines is that they're supposed to cook low and slow. We count on that when we flip the switch in the morning before we leave the house for ten hours or so. So, because none of us knows what kind of temperament our slow cooker has until we try it out, nor how hot it cooks—don't assume anything. Save yourself a disappointment and make the first recipe in your new slow cooker on a day when you're at home. Cook it for the shortest amount of time the recipe calls for. Then, check the food to see if it's done. Or if you start smelling food that seems to be finished, turn off the cooker and rescue your food.

Also, all slow cookers seem to have a "hot spot," which is of great importance to know, especially when baking with your slow cooker. This spot may tend to burn food in that area if you're not careful. If you're baking directly in your slow cooker, I recommend covering the "hot spot" with some foil.

Take Notes . . .

Don't be afraid to make notes in your cookbook. It's yours! Chances are, it will eventually get passed down to someone in your family and they will love and appreciate all of your musings. Take note of which slow cooker you used and exactly how long it took to cook the recipe. The next time you make it, you won't need to try to remember. Apply what you learned to the next recipes you make in your cooker. If another recipe says it needs to cook for 7 to 9 hours, and you've discovered your slow cooker cooks on the faster side, cook that recipe for 6 to 6½ hours and then check it. You can always cook a recipe longer—but you can't reverse things if it's overdone.

Get Creative . . .

If you know your morning is going to be hectic, prepare everything the night before, take it out so the crock warms up to room temperature when you first get up in the morning, then plug it in and turn it on as you're leaving the house.

If you want to make something that has a short cook time and you're going to be gone longer than that, cook it the night before and refrigerate it for the next day. Warm it up when you get home. Or, cook those recipes on the weekend when you know you'll be home and eat them later in the week.

Slow-Cooker Tips and Tricks and Other Things You May Not Know

- Slow cookers tend to work best when they're ⅔ to ¾ of the way full. You may need to increase the cooking time if you've exceeded that amount, or reduce it if you've put in less than that. If you're going to exceed that limit, it would be best to reduce the recipe, or split it between two slow cookers. (Remember how I suggested owning at least two or three slow cookers?)

- Keep your veggies on the bottom. That puts them in more direct contact with the heat. The fuller your slow cooker, the longer it will take its contents to cook. Also, the more densely packed the cooker's contents are, the longer they will take to cook. And finally, the larger the chunks of meat or vegetables, the more time they will need to cook.

- Keep the lid on! Every time you take a peek, you lose 20 minutes of cooking time. Please take this into consideration each time you lift the lid! I know, some of you can't help yourself and are going to lift anyway. Just don't forget to tack on 20 minutes to your cook time for each time you peeked!

- Sometimes it's beneficial to remove the lid. If you'd like your dish to thicken a bit, take the lid off during the last half hour to hour of cooking time.
- If you have a big slow cooker (7- to 8-quart), you can cook a small batch in it by putting the recipe ingredients into an oven-safe baking dish or baking pan and then placing that into the cooker's crock. First, put a trivet or some metal jar rings on the bottom of the crock, and then set your dish or pan on top of them. Or a loaf pan may "hook onto" the top ridges of the crock belonging to a large oval cooker and hang there straight and securely, "baking" a cake or quick bread. Cover the cooker and flip it on.
- The outside of your slow cooker will be hot! Please remember to keep it out of reach of children and keep that in mind for yourself as well!
- Get yourself a quick-read meat thermometer and use it! This helps remove the question of whether or not your meat is fully cooked, and helps prevent you from overcooking your meat as well.
  - Internal Cooking Temperatures: Beef—125–130°F (rare); 140–145°F (medium); 160°F (well-done)
  - Pork—140–145°F (rare); 145–150°F (medium); 160°F (well-done)
  - Turkey and Chicken—165°F
  - Frozen meat: The basic rule of thumb is, don't put frozen meat into the slow cooker. The meat does not reach the proper internal temperature in time. This especially applies to thick cuts of meat! Proceed with caution!
- Add fresh herbs 10 minutes before the end of the cooking time to maximize their flavor.
- If your recipe calls for cooked pasta, add it 10 minutes before the end of the cooking time if the cooker is on High; 30 minutes before the end of the cooking time if it's on low. Then the pasta won't get mushy.
- If your recipe calls for sour cream or cream, stir it in 5 minutes before the end of the cooking time. You want it to heat but not boil or simmer.
- Approximate Slow-Cooker Temperatures (Remember, each slow cooker is different):
  - High—212°F–300°F
  - Low—170°F–200°F
  - Simmer—185°F
  - Warm—165°F
- Cooked beans freeze well. Store them in freezer bags (squeeze the air out first) or freezer boxes. Cooked and dried bean measurements:
  - 16-oz. can, drained = about 1¾ cups beans
  - 19-oz. can, drained = about 2 cups beans
  - 1 lb. dried beans (about 2½ cups) = 5 cups cooked beans

What Is an Instant Pot?

In short, an Instant Pot is a digital pressure cooker that also has multiple other functions. Not only can it be used as a pressure cooker, but depending on which model Instant Pot you have, you can set it to do things like sauté, cook rice, grains, porridge, soup/stew, beans/chili, porridge, meat, poultry, cake, eggs, yogurt. You can use the Instant Pot to steam or slow cook or even set it manually. Because the Instant Pot has so many functions, it takes away the need for multiple appliances on your counter and allows you to use fewer pots and pans.

Getting Started with Your Instant Pot

Get to Know Your Instant Pot . . .

The very first thing most Instant Pot owners do is called the water test. It helps you get to know your Instant Pot a bit, familiarizes you with it, and might even take a bit of your apprehension away (because if you're anything like me, I was scared to death to use it).

Step 1: Plug in your Instant Pot. This may seem obvious to some, but when we're nervous about using a new appliance, sometimes we forget things like this.

Step 2: Make sure the inner pot is inserted in the cooker. You should *never* attempt to cook anything in your device without the inner pot, or you will ruin your Instant Pot. Food should never come into contact with the actual housing unit.

Step 3: The inner pot has lines for each cup. Fill the inner pot with water until it reaches the 3-cup line.

Step 4: Check the sealing ring to be sure it's secure and in place. You should not be able to move it around. If it's not in place properly, you may experience issues with the pot letting out a lot of steam while cooking, or not coming to pressure.

Step 5: Seal the lid. There is an arrow on the lid between Open and Close. There is also an arrow on the top of the base of the Instant Pot between a picture of a locked lock and an unlocked lock. Line those arrows up, then turn the lid toward the picture of the lock (left).You will hear a noise that will indicate the lid is locked. If you do not hear a noise, it's not locked. Try it again.

Step 6: *Always* check to see if the steam valve on top of the lid is turned to Sealing. If it's not on Sealing and is on Venting, it will not be able to come to pressure.

Step 7: Press the Steam button and use the +/- arrow to set it to 2 minutes. Once it's at the desired time, you don't need to press anything else. In a few seconds, the Instant Pot will begin all on its own. For those of us with digital slow cookers, we have a tendency to look for the "start" button, but there isn't one on the Instant Pot.

Step 8: Now you wait for the "magic" to happen! The cooking will begin once the device comes to pressure. This can take anywhere from 5 to 30 minutes, in my experience. Then, you will see the countdown happen (from the time you set it for). After that, the Instant Pot will beep, which means your meal is done!

Step 9: Your Instant Pot will now automatically switch to Warm and begin a count of how many minutes it's been on warm. The next part is where you either wait for the NPR, or natural pressure release (the pressure releases on its own) or do what's called a QR, or quick release (you manually release the pressure). Which method you choose depends on what you're cooking, but in this case, you can choose either, because it's just water. For NPR, you will wait for the lever to move all the way back over to Venting and watch the pinion (float valve) next to the lever. It will be flush with the lid when at full pressure and will drop when the pressure is done releasing. If you choose QR, be very careful not to have your hands over the vent, as the steam is very hot and you can burn yourself.

The Three Most Important Buttons You Need to Know About

You will find the majority of recipes will use the following three buttons:

Manual/Pressure Cook: Some older models tend to say Manual, and the newer models seem to say Pressure Cook. They mean the same thing. From here, you use the +/- button to change the cook time. After several seconds, the Instant Pot will begin its process. The exact name of this button will vary on your model of Instant Pot.

Saute: Many recipes will have you sauté vegetables, or brown meat before beginning the pressure cooking process. For this setting, you will not use the lid of the Instant Pot.

Keep Warm/Cancel: This may just be the most important button on the Instant Pot. When you forget to use the +/- buttons to change the time for a recipe, or you press a wrong button, you can hit Keep Warm/Cancel and it will turn your Instant Pot off for you.

What Do All the Buttons Do?

With so many buttons, it's hard to remember what each one does or means. You can use this as a quick guide in a pinch.

Soup/Broth. This button cooks at high pressure for 30 minutes. It can be adjusted using the +/- buttons to cook more, for 40 minutes, or less, for 20 minutes.

Meat/Stew. This button cooks at high pressure for 35 minutes. It can be adjusted using the +/- buttons to cook more, for 45 minutes, or less, for 20 minutes.

Bean/Chili. This button cooks at high pressure for 30 minutes. It can be adjusted using the +/- buttons to cook more, for 40 minutes, or less, for 25 minutes.

Poultry. This button cooks at high pressure for 15 minutes. It can be adjusted using the +/- buttons to cook more, for 30 minutes, or less, for 5 minutes.

Rice. This button cooks at low pressure and is the only fully automatic program. It is for cooking white rice and will automatically adjust the cooking time depending on the amount of water and rice in the cooking pot.

Multigrain. This button cooks at high pressure for 40 minutes. It can be adjusted using the +/- buttons to cook more, for 45 minutes of warm water soaking time and 60 minutes pressure cooking time, or less, for 20 minutes.

Porridge. This button cooks at high pressure for 20 minutes. It can be adjusted using the +/- buttons to cook more, for 30 minutes, or less, for 15 minutes.

Steam. This button cooks at High pressure for 10 minutes. It can be adjusted using the +/- buttons to cook more, for 15 minutes, or less, for 3 minutes. Always use a rack or steamer basket with this function, because it heats at full power continuously while it's coming to pressure, and you do not want food in direct contact with the bottom of the pressure cooking pot or it will burn. Once it reaches pressure, the steam button regulates pressure by cycling on and off, similar to the other pressure buttons.

Less | Normal | More. Adjust between the *Less | Normal | More* settings by pressing the same cooking function button repeatedly until you get to the desired setting. (Older versions use the *Adjust* button.)

+/- Buttons. Adjust the cook time up [+] or down [-]. (On newer models, you can also press and hold [-] or [+] for 3 seconds to turn sound OFF or ON.)

Cake. This button cooks at high pressure for 30 minutes. It can be adjusted using the +/- buttons to cook more, for 40 minutes, or less, for 25 minutes.

Egg. This button cooks at high pressure for 5 minutes. It can be adjusted using the +/- buttons to cook more, for 6 minutes, or less, for 4 minutes.

Instant Pot Tips and Tricks and Other Things You May Not Know

- Never attempt to cook directly in the Instant Pot without the inner pot!

- Once you set the time, you can walk away. It will show the time you set it to, then will change to the word "on" while the pressure builds. Once the Instant Pot has come to pressure, you will once again see the time you set it for. It will count down from there.

- Always make sure the sealing ring is securely in place. If it shows signs of wear or tear, it needs to be replaced.

- Have a sealing ring for savory recipes and a separate sealing ring for sweet recipes. Many people report their desserts tasting like a roast (or another savory food) if they try to use the same sealing ring for all recipes.

- The stainless steel rack (trivet) the Instant Pot comes with can be used to keep food from being completely submerged in liquid, like baked potatoes or ground beef. It can also be used to set another pot on, for pot-in-pot cooking.

- If you use warm or hot liquid instead of cold liquid, you may need to adjust the cooking time, or the food may not come out done.

- Always double-check to see that the valve on the lid is set to Sealing and not Venting when you first lock the lid. This will save you from the Instant Pot not coming to pressure.

- Use Natural Pressure Release for tougher cuts of meat, recipes with high starch (like rice or grains), and recipes with a high volume of liquid. This means you let the Instant Pot naturally release pressure. The little bobbin will fall once pressure is released completely.

- Use Quick Release for more delicate cuts of meat, such as seafood and chicken breasts, and for steaming vegetables. This means you manually turn the vent (being careful not to put your hand over the vent) to release the pressure. The little bobbin will fall once pressure is released completely.

- Make sure there is a clear pathway for the steam to release. The last thing you want is to ruin the bottom of your cupboards with all that steam.

- You *must* use liquid in the Instant Pot. The *minimum* amount of liquid you should have in the inner pot is ½ cup, but most recipes work best with at least 1 cup.

- Do *not* overfill the Instant Pot! It should only be ½ full for rice or beans (food that expands greatly when cooked,) or ⅔ of the way full for almost everything else. Do not fill it to the max fill line.

- In this book, the Cook Time *does not* take into account the amount of time it will take the Instant Pot to come to pressure, or the amount of time it will take the Instant Pot to release pressure. Be aware of this when choosing a recipe to make.

- If the Instant Pot is not coming to pressure, it's usually because the sealing ring is not on properly, or the vent is not set to Sealing.

- The more liquid, or the colder the ingredients, the longer it will take for the Instant Pot to come to pressure.

- Always make sure that the Instant Pot is dry before inserting the inner pot, and make sure the inner pot is dry before inserting it into the Instant Pot.
- Use a binder clip to hold the inner pot tight against the outer pot when sautéing and stirring. This will keep the pot from "spinning" in the base.
- Doubling a recipe does not change the cook time, but instead it will take longer to come up to pressure.
- You do not always need to double the liquid when doubling a recipe. Depending on what you're making, more liquid may make the food too watery. Use your best judgment.
- When using the Slow Cooker function, use the following chart:

Slow Cooker	Instant Pot
Warm	Less or Low
Low	Normal or Medium
High	More or High

Instant Pot Accessories

Most Instant Pots come with a stainless steel trivet. Below, you will find a list of common accessories that are frequently used in most Fix-It and Forget-It Instant Pot cookbooks. Most of these accessories can be purchased in-store or online.

- Steamer basket—stainless steel or silicone
- 7-inch nonstick or silicone springform or cake pan
- Sling or trivet with handles
- 1½-quart round baking dish
- Silicone egg molds

Appetizers & Snacks

Hummus

Colleen Heatwole, Burton, MI

Makes 8 servings
Prep. Time: 15 minutes   Cooking Time: 40 minutes

1 cup dry chickpeas

4 cups water

1¼ cups cottage cheese

2 Tbsp. fresh lemon juice

¼ cup chopped onion

3 cloves garlic, minced

½ cup tahini (sesame paste)

2 tsp. olive oil

2 tsp. cumin

Pinch cayenne pepper

½ tsp. salt

½ cup reserved chickpea cooking liquid

Serving suggestions:

Serve with your favorite fresh veggie, or grilled chicken slices.

1. Place chickpeas and 4 cups water into inner pot of Instant Pot. Secure lid and make sure vent is set to sealing.

2. Cook chickpeas and water for 40 minutes using the manual high-pressure setting.

3. When cooking time is up, let the pressure release naturally.

4. Test the chickpeas. If still firm, cook using slow-cooker function until they are soft.

5. Drain the chickpeas, but save ½ cup of the cooking liquid.

6. Combine the chickpeas, cottage cheese, lemon juice, onion, garlic, tahini, oil, cumin, pepper, and salt in a blender or food processor.

7. Puree until smooth, adding chickpea liquid as needed to thin the puree. Taste and adjust seasonings accordingly.

Protein: 12 g

Sweet-and-Hot Mixed Nuts

Hope Comerford, Clinton Township, MI

Makes 22 servings (about ¼ cup each)
Prep. Time: 15 minutes   Cooking Time: 2 hours
Cooling Time: 1 hour   Ideal slow-cooker size: 2- or 3-qt.

I cup unsalted cashews

I cup unsalted almonds

I cup unsalted pecans

I cup unsalted, shelled pistachios

½ cup maple syrup

⅓ cup melted coconut oil

I tsp. ground ginger

½ tsp. sea salt

½ tsp. cinnamon

¼ tsp. ground cloves

¼ tsp. cayenne pepper

1. Spray crock with nonstick cooking spray.

2. Place nuts in the crock and combine them with all the remaining ingredients, making sure all nuts are coated evenly.

3. Before covering the crock, place a piece of paper towel or thin dish towel under the lid. Cook on low for 1 hour and then stir the nuts. At 2 hours, stir again and then lay them on a parchment paper–lined cookie sheet. Let them cool for 1 hour.

4. Serve or store any remaining nuts in a covered container for up to 3 weeks.

Protein: 4 g

Lightened-Up Spinach Artichoke Dip

Hope Comerford, Clinton Township, MI

Makes 6–8 servings
Prep. Time: 10 minutes ❧ Cooking Time: 3–4 hours ❧ Ideal slow-cooker size: 3- or 4-qt.

10-oz. bag fresh baby spinach, coarsely chopped

13.75-oz. can quartered artichoke hearts, drained and chopped

8-oz. brick reduced-fat cream cheese

1 cup nonfat plain Greek yogurt

1 cup shredded mozzarella cheese

½ cup grated Parmesan cheese

½ cup chopped onion

¼ cup chopped green onion

1. Spray the crock with nonstick cooking spray.

2. Combine all ingredients in crock, making sure everything is well-mixed.

3. Cover and cook on low for 3 to 4 hours, or until the cheese is melted and the dip is heated all the way through.

Serving suggestion:

Serve with high-protein crackers, Ezekial bread, or fresh carrot sticks.

Protein: 18 g

Seven-Layer Dip

Hope Comerford, Clinton Township, MI

Makes 10–15 servings
Prep. Time: 20 minutes ❧ *Cooking Time: 2 hours* ❧ *Ideal slow-cooker size: 6-qt.*

1 lb. lean ground turkey

2½ tsp. chili powder, *divided*

½ tsp. kosher salt

⅛ tsp. pepper

15-oz. can fat-free refried beans

4-oz. can diced green chilies

1 cup nonfat Greek yogurt

1 cup salsa

1 cup shredded Mexican blend cheese

2-oz. can sliced black olives

2 green onions, sliced

1. Brown the ground turkey with 1 teaspoon chili powder, salt, and pepper.

2. Meanwhile spray the crock with nonstick cooking spray.

3. Mix together 1 teaspoon chili powder with the refried beans, then spread them into a layer at the bottom of the crock.

4. Next add a layer of the diced green chilies.

5. Spread the ground turkey over the top of the green chilies.

6. Mix together the remaining ½ teaspoon chili powder with the Greek yogurt, and then spread this over the ground turkey in the crock.

7. Next, spread the salsa over the top.

8. Last, sprinkle the cheese into a layer on top and end with the black olives.

9. Cover and cook on low for 2 hours. Sprinkle the green onions on top before serving.

Serving suggestion:
Serve with protein tortilla chips.

Protein: 12 g

Prairie Fire Dip

Cheri Jantzen, Houston, TX

Makes 1¼ cups, or 10 servings
Prep. Time: 5–10 minutes ❧ *Cooking Time: 1–3 hours* ❧ *Ideal slow-cooker size: 2-qt.*

I cup fat-free vegetarian refried beans

½ cup shredded fat-free Monterey Jack cheese

¼ cup water

I Tbsp. minced onion

I clove garlic, minced

2 tsp. chili powder

Hot sauce as desired

1. Combine all ingredients in slow cooker.

2. Cover. Cook on high for 1 hour, or on low for 2 to 3 hours.

Serving suggestion:

Garnish with diced avocado. Serve with protein tortilla chips.

Protein: 3 g

Tempting Tiny Turkey Meatballs

SLOW COOKER

Hope Comerford, Clinton Township, MI

Makes 40–50 tiny meatballs

Prep. Time: 30 minutes ❧ *Cooking Time: 6 hours* ❧ *Ideal slow-cooker size: 6- or 7-qt.*

2 lb. lean ground turkey

⅔ cup cooked quinoa

6 clove garlic, minced, *divided*

1 egg, lightly beaten

2 Tbsp. grated Parmesan

3 Tbsp. Italian seasoning, *divided*

3 tsp. onion powder, *divided*

1¾ tsp. kosher salt, *divided*

1 tsp. pepper, *divided*

4 Tbsp. olive oil, *divided*

2 (28-oz.) cans low-sodium crushed tomatoes

6-oz. can low-sodium tomato paste

¼ cup balsamic vinegar

1. Mix together the ground turkey, quinoa, 3 cloves minced garlic, egg, Parmesan cheese, 1 tablespoon Italian seasoning, 1 teaspoon onion powder, ¾ teaspoon kosher salt, and ½ teaspoon pepper. Form this into tiny ½-inch meatballs.

2. In a large skillet over medium-high heat, heat 2 tablespoons of olive oil and gently sear all sides of each meatball. Set them aside.

3. In a large bowl, mix the crushed tomatoes, tomato paste, remaining 3 cloves of minced garlic, 2 tablespoons Italian seasoning, 2 teaspoons onion powder, 1 teaspoon kosher salt, ½ teaspoon pepper, 2 tablespoons olive oil, and ¼ cup balsamic vinegar.

4. Pour half the tomato sauce mixture into the crock; gently add all the tiny meatballs. Finish by pouring the rest of the tomato sauce over the top.

5. Cover and cook on low for 6 hours.

Protein: 6 g

Chicken Lettuce Wraps

Hope Comerford, Clinton Township, MI

Makes About 12 wraps

Prep. Time: 15 minutes ❧ *Cooking Time: 2–3 hours* ❧ *Ideal slow-cooker size: 5- or 7-qt.*

2 lb. ground chicken, browned

4 cloves garlic, minced

½ cup minced sweet yellow onion

4 Tbsp. gluten-free soy sauce or Bragg Liquid Aminos

1 Tbsp. natural crunchy peanut butter

1 tsp. rice wine vinegar

1 tsp. sesame oil

¼ tsp. kosher salt

¼ tsp. red pepper flakes

¼ tsp. black pepper

8-oz. can sliced water chestnuts, drained, rinsed, chopped

3 green onions, sliced

12 good-sized pieces of iceberg lettuce, rinsed and patted dry

1. In the crock, combine the ground chicken, garlic, yellow onion, soy sauce, peanut butter, vinegar, sesame oil, salt, red pepper flakes, and black pepper.

2. Cover and cook on low for 2 to 3 hours.

3. Add the water chestnuts and green onions. Cover and cook for an additional 10 to 15 minutes.

4. Serve a good spoonful on each piece of iceberg lettuce.

Protein: 15 g

Breakfasts

Slow-Cooker Yogurt

Becky Fixel, Grosse Pointe Farms, MI

Makes 12–14 servings

Prep. Time: 2 minutes ❧ *Cooking Time: 12–14 hours* ❧ *Ideal slow-cooker size: 6-qt.*

1 gallon whole milk

5.3 oz. Greek yogurt with cultures

1. Empty the gallon of whole milk into the slow cooker and put it on high heat for 2 to 4 hours. Length of time depends on the model, but the milk needs to heat to just below boiling point, about 180°F to 200°F.

2. Turn off the slow cooker and let the milk cool down to 110°F to 115°F. Again, this will take 2 to 4 hours. Set the starter Greek yogurt out so it can reach room temperature during this step.

3. In a small bowl, add about 1 cup of the warm milk and the Greek yogurt and mix. Pour the mixture into the milk in the slow cooker and mix it in by stirring back and forth. Replace the lid of the slow cooker and wrap the whole thing in a towel. Let sit for 12 to 14 hours, or in other words, go to bed.

4. After 12 hours, check on the glorious yogurt!

5. Line a colander with cheesecloth and place in bowl. Scoop the yogurt inside and let it sit for at least 4 hours. This will help separate the extra whey from the yogurt and thicken the final yogurt.

Protein: 10 g

SLOW COOKER

Soy-Flax Granola

Phyllis Good, Lancaster, PA

Makes 15 servings

Prep. Time: 20 minutes · *Cooking Time: 2–3 hours*
Chilling Time: 2 hours · *Ideal slow-cooker size: 6-qt.*

12 oz. soybeans, roasted with no salt
4 cups gluten-free rolled oats
¾ cup soy flour
¾ cup ground flaxseeds
1 tsp. salt
2 tsp. cinnamon
1⅓ cups coarsely chopped nuts
¾ cup honey
½ cup coconut oil, melted
¾ cup unsweetened applesauce
2 tsp. vanilla extract

Optional Additions

Dried cranberries
Dried cherries
Chopped dried apricots
Chopped dried figs
Raisins

1. Grease interior of slow-cooker crock.
2. Briefly process soybeans in a blender or food processor until coarsely chopped. Place in large bowl.
3. Add oats, flour, flaxseeds, salt, cinnamon, and nuts. Mix thoroughly with spoon.
4. In a smaller bowl, combine honey, coconut oil, unsweetened applesauce, and vanilla well.
5. Pour wet ingredients over dry. Stir well, remembering to stir up from the bottom, using either a strong spoon or your clean hands.
6. Pour mixture into crock. Cover, but vent the lid by propping it open with a chopstick or wooden spoon handle. Or if you're using an oval cooker, turn the lid sideways.
7. Cook on high for 1 hour, stirring up from the bottom and around the sides every 20 minutes or so. (Set a timer so you don't forget!)
8. Switch the cooker to low. Bake for another 1 to 2 hours, still stirring every 20 minutes.
9. Granola is done when it eventually browns a bit and looks dry.
10. Pour granola onto parchment paper or a large baking sheet to cool and crisp up more.
11. Stir in any of the dried fruits that you want.
12. If you like clumps, no need to stir granola again while it cools. Otherwise, break up the granola with a spoon or your hands as it cools.
13. When completely cooled, store in airtight container.

Protein: 19 g

Grain and Fruit Cereal

Cynthia Haller, New Holland, PA

Makes 4–5 servings
Prep. Time: 5 minutes ❧ Cooking Time: 3 hours ❧ Ideal slow-cooker size: 4-qt.

⅓ cup uncooked quinoa

⅓ cup uncooked millet

⅓ cup uncooked brown rice

4 cups water

¼ tsp. salt

½ cup raisins or dried cranberries

¼ cup chopped nuts, *optional*

I tsp. vanilla extract, *optional*

½ tsp. ground cinnamon, *optional*

I Tbsp. maple syrup, *optional*

1. Wash the quinoa, millet, and brown rice and rinse well.

2. Place the grains, water, and salt in a slow cooker. Cook on low until most of the water has been absorbed, about 3 hours.

3. Add dried fruit and any optional ingredients, and cook for 30 minutes more. If the mixture is too thick, add a little more water.

4. Serve hot or cold.

Serving suggestion:

Add a little milk to each bowl of cereal before serving.

Tip:

For extra protein, stir in a scoop of whey protein powder or a dollop of Greek yogurt.

Protein: 5 g

Overnight Oat Groats

Rebekah Zehr, Lowville, NY

Makes 6 servings
Prep. Time: 5 minutes ❧ *Cooking Time: 8–10 hours* ❧ *Ideal slow-cooker size: 3-qt.*

1½ cups gluten-free oat groats

4 cups water

2 cups almond milk

1–2 cinnamon sticks

⅓ cup maple syrup

½–1 cup dried apples

2 scoops gluten-free vanilla-flavored protein powder

1. Combine all ingredients in slow cooker.

2. Cook on low for 8 to 10 hours.

3. Remove cinnamon sticks and serve while warm.

Protein: 13 g

Five-Grain Slow Cooker Breakfast

Dena Mell-Dorchy, Royal Oak, MI

Makes 8 servings
Prep. Time: 15 minutes   ❧   *Cooking Time: 6–7 hours*   ❧   *Ideal slow-cooker size: 3- or 4-qt.*

5 cups of water

1 cup of dried fruit and nuts
(cranberries, cherries, raisins, pineapple,
coconut, pecans, and/or walnuts)

¼ cup crystallized ginger

3 Tbsp. gluten-free oats

3 Tbsp. quinoa

3 Tbsp. brown rice

2 Tbsp. flaxseeds

2 Tbsp. gluten-free cornmeal

1 tsp. vanilla extract

1 tsp. cinnamon

1 Tbsp. hemp seeds

Optional Toppings

Milk

Greek yogurt

Turbinado sugar

Maple syrup

Honey

1. Spray slow cooker with nonstick cooking spray.

2. Combine all ingredients (except optional toppings) in slow cooker, cover, and cook on low for 6 to 7 hours.

3. Serve with any of the optional toppings, if desired.

Protein: 4 g

Warm 'n' Fruity

Marlene Weaver, Lititz, PA

Makes 10 cups, 1 cup/serving
Prep. Time: 10 minutes 🍃 Cooking Time: 6–7 hours 🍃 Ideal slow-cooker size: 5-qt.

5 cups water

2 cups seven-grain cereal

1 medium apple, peeled and chopped

1 cup unsweetened apple juice

¼ cup dried apricots, chopped

¼ cup dried cranberries

¼ cup raisins

¼ cup chopped dates

¼ cup maple syrup

1 tsp. cinnamon

½ tsp. salt

1¼ cup chopped walnuts, *divided*

¾ cup Greek yogurt

1. In the crock, combine all ingredients except for walnuts and Greek yogurt.

2. Cover and cook on low for 6 to 7 hours or until fruits are softened.

3. Top each serving with 2 tablespoons chopped walnuts and approximately 1 tablespoon Greek yogurt.

Protein: 9 g

Sweet Potatoes Ole

Hope Comerford, Clinton Township, MI

Makes 8 servings
Prep. Time: 10 minutes   &   Cooking Time: 6 hours   &   Ideal slow-cooker size: 5- or 6-qt.

4 lb. sweet potatoes, peeled and diced

15-oz. can black beans, drained, rinsed

1 cup chopped onion

4-oz. can diced green chilies

8 eggs

½ cup salsa

½ cup shredded Monterey Jack cheese

1. Spray crock with nonstick cooking spray.

2. In crock, mix the sweet potatoes, black beans, onion, and diced green chilies.

3. In a bowl, mix the eggs, salsa, and Monterey Jack cheese. Pour over the sweet potatoes.

4. Cover and cook on low for 6 hours.

Protein: 16 g

Fiesta Hash Browns

Dena Mell-Dorchy, Royal Oak, MI

Makes 8 servings
Prep. Time: 15 minutes Cooking Time: 8–9 hours Ideal slow-cooker size: 3- or 4-qt.

1 lb. ground turkey sausage
½ cup chopped onion
5 cups frozen diced hash browns
8 oz. low-sodium chicken stock
1 small red sweet pepper
1 jalapeño, seeded and finely diced
1½ cups sliced mushrooms
2 Tbsp. quick-cooking tapioca
½ cup shredded Monterey Jack cheese

1. Spray slow cooker with nonstick cooking spray.

2. In a large skillet, brown sausage and onion over medium heat. Drain off fat.

3. Combine sausage mixture, hash browns, chicken stock, sweet pepper, jalapeño, mushrooms, and quick-cooking tapioca in cooker; stir to combine.

4. Cover and cook on low heat for 8 to 9 hours. Stir before serving. Top with shredded Monterey Jack cheese.

Protein: 18 g

Huevos Rancheros in Crock

Pat Bishop, Bedminster, PA

Makes 6 servings

Prep. Time: 25 minutes ❧ *Cooking Time: 2 hours* ❧ *Ideal slow-cooker size: 6-qt.*

3 cups salsa, room temperature

2 cups cooked beans, drained, room temperature

6 eggs, room temperature

Salt to taste

Pepper to taste

⅓ cup grated Mexican-blend cheese, *optional*

6 white corn tortillas, for serving

1. Mix salsa and beans in slow cooker.

2. Cook on high for 1 hour or until steaming.

3. With a spoon, make 6 evenly spaced dents in the salsa mixture; try not to expose the bottom of the crock. Break an egg into each dent.

4. Salt and pepper eggs. Sprinkle with cheese if you wish.

5. Cover and continue to cook on high until egg whites are set and yolks are as firm as you like them, approximately 20 to 40 minutes.

6. To serve, scoop out an egg with some beans and salsa. Serve with warm tortillas.

Protein: 15 g

Spanish Breakfast "Skillet"

Hope Comerford, Clinton Township, MI

Makes 6 servings
Prep. Time: 25 minutes & Cooking Time: 5–6 hours & Ideal slow-cooker size: 5- or 6-qt.

I lb. turkey sausage, browned, drained

4.5-oz. pkg. tostada shells, broken coarsely

I medium red bell pepper, chopped

I medium onion, chopped

4-oz. can diced green chilies

I cup almond milk

12 eggs

I tsp. sea salt

¼ tsp. black pepper

½ cup crumbled queso fresco

Optional Toppings

2 sliced avocados

8 oz. nonfat Greek yogurt

2 cups salsa

1. Spray crock with nonstick cooking spray.

2. In crock, combine browned sausage, tostada pieces, red bell pepper, onion, and green chilies.

3. In a large bowl mix together the almond milk, eggs, sea salt, and black pepper.

4. Pour egg mixture over sausage mixture in crock.

5. Sprinkle crumbled queso fresco over the top.

6. Cover and cook on low for 5 to 6 hours.

Protein: 32 g

Breakfast "Sausage" Casserole

Kendra Dreps, Liberty, PA

Makes 8 servings
Prep. Time: 15 minutes   Chilling Time: 8 hours
Cooking Time: 4 hours   Ideal slow-cooker size: 3-qt.

I lb. meatless sausage crumbles

6 eggs

2 cups milk

8 slices Ezekial bread, cubed

I cup shredded mozzarella cheese

1. In a nonstick skillet, brown sausage crumbles.

2. Mix eggs and milk in a large bowl.

3. Stir in bread cubes, cheese, and sausage.

4. Place in greased slow cooker.

5. Refrigerate overnight.

6. Cook on low for 4 hours.

Protein: 30 g

Baked Eggs

Esther J. Mast, Lancaster, PA

Makes 8 servings

Prep. Time: 15 minutes   *Cooking Time: 20 minutes*   *Standing Time: 10 minutes*

1 cup water

2 Tbsp. soft margarine, melted

1 cup buttermilk baking mix

1 ½ cups cottage cheese

2 tsp. chopped onion

1 tsp. dried parsley

Salt

½ cup shredded reduced-fat cheddar cheese

1 egg, slightly beaten

1 ¼ cups egg substitute

1 cup fat-free milk

1. Place the trivet into the bottom of the inner pot and pour in the water.

2. Grease a round 7-inch springform pan that will fit into the inner pot of the Instant Pot.

3. Pour the melted margarine into the springform pan.

4. In a large mixing bowl, mix the buttermilk baking mix, cottage cheese, onion, parsley, salt, cheese, egg, egg substitute, and milk.

5. Pour the mixture over the melted margarine. Stir slightly to distribute the margarine.

6. Place the springform pan onto the trivet, close the lid, and secure to the locking position. Be sure the vent is turned to sealing. Set for 20 minutes on Manual at high pressure.

7. Let the pressure release naturally.

8. Carefully remove the springform pan with the handles of the steaming rack and allow to stand 10 minutes before cutting and serving.

Serving suggestion:

Serve with a fresh fruit cup.

Protein: 15 g

Spinach and Mushroom Frittata

J. B. Miller, Indianapolis, IN

Makes 4 servings

Prep. Time: 5 minutes ❧ *Cooking Time: 10 minutes*

6 eggs

½ tsp. salt

¼ tsp. black pepper

1 Tbsp. fresh basil, minced

3 cloves garlic, minced

1 small shallot, minced

½ lb. sliced baby bella mushrooms

10-oz. bag fresh spinach

¼ cup shredded Gruyère cheese

1 cup water

1. In a bowl, beat the eggs, salt, and pepper.

2. Gently fold in the basil, garlic, shallot, mushrooms, spinach, and cheese.

3. Spray a 7-inch round pan with nonstick cooking spray, then pour in the egg/vegetable/cheese mixture.

4. Pour the water into the bottom of the inner pot of the Instant Pot.

5. Place the 7-inch round pan on top of the trivet and slowly lower it into the Instant Pot using the handles.

6. Secure the lid and set the valve to sealing.

7. Set the Instant Pot to Manual and set the cooking time to 10 minutes.

8. When the cooking time is over, let the pressure release naturally, then remove the lid and remove the trivet and pan carefully with oven mitts.

9. Slice into 4 slices and serve warm.

Serving suggestion:

Serve alongside a slice of Ezekial bread and a bowl of fruit.

Protein: 16 g

To-Go Crustless Veggie-Packed Quiche Cups

Hope Comerford, Clinton Township, MI

Makes 14 mini quiches

Prep. Time: 15 minutes   Cooking Time: 11 minutes   Cooling Time: 5 minutes

2 tsp. olive oil

½ green bell pepper, diced

¼ cup finely chopped broccoli florets

½ small onion, diced

5 oz. fresh spinach

8 eggs

¼ cup skim milk

3 drops hot sauce, *optional*

⅓ cup shredded mozzarella cheese

I cup water

1. Press Saute. Heat 2 teaspoons olive oil over medium-high heat.

2. Sauté the bell pepper, broccoli, and onion for about 8 minutes. Add the spinach and continue to cook until wilted.

3. Spray 2 egg molds with nonstick cooking spray. Divide the cooked vegetables evenly between the egg bite mold cups.

Serving suggestion:

Serve alongside a slice of Ezekial bread and a bowl of fruit.

4. In a bowl, whisk the eggs, skim milk, and hot sauce (if using). Divide this evenly between the egg bite mold cups, or until each cup is ⅔ of the way full. Cover them tightly with foil.

5. Evenly divide the shredded cheese between the cups.

6. Pour the water into the inner pot of the Instant Pot. Gently scrape the bottom with a wooden spoon to make sure there are no browned bits from the vegetables stuck to the bottom. Press Cancel.

7. Place the trivet into the pot, then place the 2 filled egg bite molds on top of the trivet, the top one stacked staggered on top of the one below.

8. Secure the lid and set the vent to sealing.

9. Manually set the cook time for 11 minutes on high pressure.

10. When the cook time is up, let the pressure release naturally for 5 minutes, then manually release the remaining pressure.

11. When the pin drops, remove the lid and carefully lift the trivet and molds out with oven mitts.

12. Place the molds on a wire rack and uncover. Let cool for about 5 minutes, then pop them out onto a plate or serving platter.

Protein: 17 g

Crustless Spinach Quiche

Barbara Hoover, Landisville, PA

Makes 8 servings

Prep. Time: 15 minutes ⚬ *Cooking Time: 2–4 hours* ⚬ *Ideal slow-cooker size: 3- or 4-qt.*

2 (10-oz.) pkg. frozen chopped spinach

2 cups low-fat cottage cheese

¼ cup coconut oil

1½ cups reduced-fat sharp cheddar cheese, cubed

3 eggs, beaten

¼ cup all-purpose flour

1 tsp. kosher salt

1. Grease interior of slow-cooker crock.

2. Thaw spinach completely. Squeeze as dry as you can. Then place in crock.

3. Stir in all other ingredients and combine well.

4. Cover. Cook on low for 2 to 4 hours, or until quiche is set. Stick blade of knife into center of quiche. If blade comes out clean, quiche is set. If it doesn't, cover and cook another 15 minutes or so.

5. When cooked, allow to stand 10 to 15 minutes so mixture can firm up, then serve.

Serving suggestion:

Serve with a slice of Ezekial bread and a bowl of fresh fruit.

Protein: 17 g

Soups, Stews & Chilis

Chicken & Turkey

Chicken and Vegetable Soup

Hope Comerford, Clinton Township, MI

Makes 4–6 servings

Prep. Time: 15 minutes   Cooking Time: 7–8 hours   Ideal slow-cooker size: 5-qt.

1 lb. boneless, skinless chicken, cut into bite-size pieces

2 celery ribs, diced

1 small yellow squash, diced

4 oz. sliced mushrooms

2 large carrots, diced

1 medium onion, chopped

2 Tbsp. garlic powder

1 Tbsp. onion powder

1 Tbsp. basil

½ tsp. no-salt seasoning

1 tsp. salt

Black pepper to taste

32 oz. low-sodium chicken stock

1. Place the chicken, vegetables, and spices into the crock. Pour the chicken stock over the top.

2. Cover and cook on low for 7 to 8 hours, or until vegetables are tender.

Serving suggestions:

- For a bit of extra added protein, sprinkle each bowl with 1 tablespoon nutritional yeast.
- Sprinkle with fresh parsley before serving.

Protein: 28 g

Chicken Noodle Soup

Hope Comerford, Clinton Township, MI

Makes 7 servings
Prep. Time: 10 minutes & Cooking Time: 30 minutes

2 lb. whole chicken, skin removed

3 medium carrots, sliced

1 large onion, skin removed, but left whole

½ tsp. pepper

1 bay leaf

1 tsp. oregano

½ tsp. basil

2 tsp. salt

32 oz. low-sodium chicken stock

6 cups water (or enough to just reach the fill line)

8 oz. uncooked protein pasta of your choice

1. Place the chicken, carrots, onion, pepper, bay leaf, oregano, basil, salt, chicken stock, and water (enough to fill the inner pot to the fill line) in the inner pot of the Instant Pot.

2. Secure the lid and set the vent to sealing.

3. Set the cook time manually to 30 minutes on high pressure.

4. When the cooking time is over, manually release the pressure.

5. Remove and discard the onion and bay leaf.

6. Carefully remove the chicken from the pot and remove the meat from the bones, discarding the bones. Shred the meat as best you can and place back in inner pot.

7. Add the noodles of your choice, secure the lid back on, and turn the Instant Pot to Keep Warm. Let the noodles cook for about 15 minutes. If you are using noodles that have a fast cook time, check on them sooner.

Tip:

If you plan to have leftovers, you may consider skipping step 7. Instead, you can cook the noodles on the stove, then place the desired amount of cooked noodles in each bowl and spoon the chicken soup over the noodles for each serving.

Protein: 36 g

Chicken Barley Soup

Ida H. Goering, Dayton, VA

Makes 6 servings
Prep. Time: 8–11 minutes   Cooking Time: 18 minutes

2 Tbsp. olive oil

2½ medium carrots, diced

3 celery ribs, diced

1 small onion, chopped

1 lb. boneless, skinless chicken, chopped

¾ cup uncooked pearl barley

14.5-oz. can no-salt-added diced tomatoes

½ tsp. black pepper

1 bay leaf

6 cups low-sodium chicken stock

2 Tbsp. chopped fresh parsley

1. Set the Instant Pot to Saute and heat the olive oil.

2. When the oil is heated, sauté the carrots, celery, and onion for about 3 minutes, then add the chicken and sauté for an additional 5 to 8 minutes, or until lightly browned.

3. Press Cancel and add the pearl barley, tomatoes, pepper, bay leaf, and chicken stock to the inner pot.

4. Secure the lid and set the vent to sealing.

5. Manually set the time for 18 minutes on high pressure.

6. When the cooking time is over, let the pressure release naturally.

7. Remove bay leaf and serve with a sprinkle of fresh chopped parsley in each bowl.

Protein: 27 g

Spicy Chicken Soup with Edamame

J. B. Miller, Indianapolis, IN

Makes 8 servings
Prep. Time: 8 minutes   Cooking Time: 20 minutes

2 Tbsp. olive oil

1 bunch (about 6) green onions, thinly sliced

1 red bell pepper, chopped

1 yellow bell pepper, chopped

2 jalapeño peppers, seeded and finely chopped

4 cloves garlic, chopped

1½ lb. boneless, skinless, chicken breasts

½ tsp. ground ginger

½ tsp. ground pepper

4 cups low-sodium chicken broth

3 cups fresh, or frozen, edamame, shelled

1. Set the Instant Pot to Saute and heat up the oil in the inner pot.

2. Sauté the green onions, bell peppers, jalapeños, and garlic in the oil for about 3 minutes. Push them to the outer edges and sear the chicken breasts on both sides.

3. Press Cancel. Add the remaining ingredients, except for the edamame, and secure the lid. Make sure the vent is set to sealing.

4. Manually set the cook time for 15 minutes on high pressure.

5. When the cooking time is over, manually release the pressure.

6. When the pin drops, remove the lid, then remove the chicken and shred it between two forks. Replace it back in the soup.

7. Stir the edamame into the soup and press Keep Warm. Allow it to cook for about 5 additional minutes, then serve.

Protein: 36 g

Chicken Tortilla Soup

Becky Fixel, Grosse Pointe Farms, MI

Makes 10–12 servings

Prep. Time: 5 minutes   ❧   *Cooking Time: 7–8 hours*   ❧   *Ideal slow-cooker size: 5-qt.*

2 lb. boneless, skinless chicken breast

32 oz. gluten-free chicken stock

14 oz. verde sauce

10-oz. can diced tomatoes with lime juice

15-oz. can sweet corn, drained

1 Tbsp. minced garlic

1 small onion, diced

1 Tbsp. chili pepper

½ tsp. fresh ground pepper

½ tsp. salt

½ tsp. oregano

1 Tbsp. dried jalapeño slices

1. Add all ingredients to the slow cooker.

2. Cook on low for 7 to 8 hours.

3. Approximately 30 minutes before the end, remove the chicken and shred it into small pieces.

Serving suggestion:

Top with a dollop of nonfat plain Greek yogurt, shredded cheese, fresh jalapeños, or fresh cilantro.

Protein: 19 g

Chicken Chickpea Tortilla Soup

Hope Comerford, Clinton Township, MI

Makes 4–6 servings
Prep. Time: 5 minutes   Cooking Time: 6 hours   Ideal slow-cooker size: 4-qt.

2 boneless, skinless chicken breasts

2 (14½-oz.) cans petite diced tomatoes

15-oz. can garbanzo beans (chickpeas), drained

6 cups low-sodium chicken stock

1 onion, chopped

4-oz. can diced green chilies

1 tsp. cilantro

3–4 fresh cloves garlic, minced

1 tsp. sea salt

1 tsp. pepper

1 tsp. cumin

1 tsp. paprika

1. Place all ingredients in slow cooker.

2. Cover and cook on low for 6 hours.

3. Remove chicken into a bowl and use two forks to pull apart chicken into shreds. Stir it back through the soup, then serve.

Serving suggestion:

Serve with a small dollop of nonfat Greek yogurt, a little reduced-fat shredded cheddar, and some protein tortilla chips.

Protein: 14 g

Sausage, Beans, and Rice Soup

Sharon Easter, Yuba City, CA

Makes 5 servings
Prep. Time: 5–8 minutes   Cooking Time: 20 minutes

I Tbsp. olive oil

½ lb. bulk turkey sausage

28-oz. can no-salt-added diced tomatoes

¼ tsp. pepper

½ tsp. dried oregano

½ cup uncooked brown rice

15-oz. can cannellini beans, rinsed and drained

6 cups low-sodium chicken stock or vegetable stock

1. Set the Instant Pot to Saute and heat the olive oil in the inner pot.

2. Sauté the turkey sausage for 5 minutes, or until lightly browned.

3. Press Cancel and then add the tomatoes, pepper, oregano, brown rice, beans, and stock to the inner pot.

4. Secure the lid and set the vent to sealing.

5. Manually set the time for 20 minutes on high pressure.

6. When the cooking time is over, let the pressure release naturally for 10 minutes, then manually release the remaining pressure.

7. Serve and enjoy!

Protein: 26 g

Chicken, Pumpkin, and Chickpea Stew

Andrea Maher, West Chester, PA

Makes 6 servings
Prep. Time: 10 minutes ❧ *Cooking Time: 3–8 hours* ❧ *Ideal slow-cooker size: 5- or 6-qt.*

24 oz. boneless, skinless chicken, cut thin

3 cups canned pumpkin puree

2 cups chickpeas

3 cups mushrooms

1½ cups gluten-free low-sodium chicken broth

1½ cups plain nonfat Greek yogurt

Salt to taste

Pepper to taste

Cinnamon to taste

Red pepper and chili powder to taste, if desired

1. Add all ingredients to slow cooker.

2. Cook on high for 3 to 4 hours or on low for 6 to 8 hours.

Tip:

This soup freezes well, so it's easy to freeze in portion-sized containers.

Protein: 46 g

Chicken Chili Pepper Stew

Susan Kasting, Jenks, OK

Makes 4 servings
Prep. Time: 5 minutes   *Cooking Time: 8 minutes*

14.5 oz. low-sodium chicken stock

1 lb. boneless, skinless chicken breasts

4 cloves garlic, minced

1–2 jalapeño peppers, seeded and diced

1 medium red bell pepper, diced

1 medium carrot, sliced

15-oz. can no-salt-added corn, drained

1 tsp. cumin

2 Tbsp. chopped cilantro

1. Place all the ingredients, except the chopped cilantro, into the inner pot of the Instant Pot and secure the lid. Set the vent to sealing.

2. Manually set the cook time for 8 minutes on high pressure.

3. When the cooking time is over, let the pressure release naturally for 5 minutes, then manually release the pressure.

4. When the pin drops, remove the lid, remove the chicken, shred between two forks, then replace back in the inner pot. Stir.

5. Serve each bowl of stew with a sprinkling of chopped cilantro.

Protein: 30 g

Southwestern Chili

Colleen Heatwole, Burton, MI

Makes 12 servings
Prep. Time: 30 minutes   Cooking Time: 6–8 hours   Ideal slow-cooker size: 6- or 7-qt.

32-oz. can whole tomatoes

15-oz. jar salsa

15-oz. can low-sodium chicken broth

1 cup barley

3 cups water

1 tsp. chili powder

1 tsp. ground cumin

15-oz. can black beans

15-oz. can whole-kernel corn

3 cups cooked chicken, chopped

1 cup low-fat shredded cheddar cheese, *optional*

Low-fat sour cream, *optional*

1. Combine all ingredients in slow cooker except for optional cheese and sour cream.

2. Cover and cook on low for 6 to 8 hours.

3. Serve with optional cheese and sour cream on each bowl.

Protein: 22 g

White and Green Chili

Hope Comerford, Clinton Township, MI

Makes 6 servings
Prep. Time: 20 minutes & Cooking Time: 7–8 hours & Ideal slow-cooker size: 4-qt.

I lb. lean ground turkey, browned

I cup chopped onion

2 (15-oz.) cans great northern beans, rinsed and drained

16-oz. jar salsa verde (choose your own spice level)

2 cups gluten-free chicken broth

4-oz. can mild green chilies

1½ tsp. ground cumin

I tsp. sea salt

¼ tsp. black pepper

2 Tbsp. fresh chopped cilantro

⅓ cup nonfat plain Greek yogurt

1. Place all ingredients in crock except cilantro and Greek yogurt. Stir.

2. Cover and cook on low for 7 to 8 hours. Stir in cilantro.

3. Serve each bowl of chili with a dollop of the Greek yogurt.

Serving suggestion:

Garnish with diced jalapeño peppers.

Protein: 29 g

Chipotle Chili

Janie Steele, Moore, OK

Makes 6–8 servings
Prep. Time: 30 minutes & Cooking Time: 3–6 hours & Ideal slow-cooker size: 3- or 4-qt.

2 cloves garlic, chopped

1 ¼ lb. boneless, skinless chicken thighs, cubed

1 lb. butternut squash, peeled and cubed

15-oz. can pinto beans, rinsed and drained

Juice and zest of ½ orange

2–3 chipotle peppers in adobo sauce, minced

2 Tbsp. tomato paste

2 green onions, sliced, chopped

Cilantro, *optional*

1. Combine garlic, chicken, squash, beans, orange juice, orange zest, peppers, and tomato paste in slow cooker.

2. Cook for 3 to 4 hours on high or 5 to 6 hours on low until chicken is done.

3. Mash some of the stew with potato masher to make it thicker.

4. Stir in green onions and optional cilantro. Serve hot.

Protein: 17 g

Pork, Beef & Lamb

Navy Bean and Ham Soup

Jennifer Freed, Rockingham, VA

Makes 6 servings
Prep. Time: Overnight, or approximately 8 hours ❧ *Cooking Time: 8–10 hours*
❧ *Ideal slow-cooker size: 6½- or 7-qt.*

6 cups water

5 cups dried navy beans, soaked overnight, drained, and rinsed

1 lb. ham, cubed

15-oz. can corn, drained

4-oz. can mild diced green chilies, drained

1 onion, diced, *optional*

Salt to taste

Pepper to taste

1. Place all ingredients in slow cooker.

2. Cover and cook on low for 8 to 10 hours, or until beans are tender.

Protein: 52 g

Beef Mushroom Barley Soup

Becky Frey, Lebanon, PA

Makes 8 servings
Prep. Time: 20 minutes   *Cooking Time: 25 minutes*

2 Tbsp. olive oil, *divided*

1 lb. boneless beef chuck, trimmed of fat, cubed

1 large onion, chopped

2 cloves garlic, crushed

1 lb. fresh mushrooms, sliced

1 celery rib, sliced

2 carrots, sliced

½ tsp. dried thyme, *optional*

8 cups low-sodium beef stock

½ cup uncooked pearl barley

½ tsp. freshly ground pepper

3 Tbsp. chopped fresh parsley

1. Set the Instant Pot to Saute and heat up 1 tablespoon of the olive oil in the inner pot.

2. Brown the beef, in batches if needed, and then remove and set aside.

3. Add the remaining tablespoon of olive oil and sauté the onion, garlic, and mushrooms for 3 to 4 minutes.

4. Add the beef back in, as well as all the remaining ingredients, except for the parsley. Press Cancel.

5. Secure the lid and set the vent to sealing.

6. Manually set the cook time to 25 minutes on high pressure.

7. When the cooking time is over, let the pressure release naturally for 15 minutes, then manually release the remaining pressure.

8. When the pin drops, remove the lid and stir. Serve each bowl topped with some fresh chopped parsley.

Protein: 20 g

Stuffed Sweet Pepper Stew

Moreen Weaver, Bath, NY

Makes 10 servings
Prep. Time: 10 minutes   *Cooking Time: 10 minutes*

1 lb. 95% lean ground beef

¼ tsp. salt

⅛ tsp. pepper

2 cloves garlic, minced

1 large onion, diced

2 quarts low-sodium tomato juice, *divided*

3 medium red, or green, bell peppers, diced

1½ cups chili sauce, no-salt-added

1 cup uncooked brown rice

2 celery ribs, diced

3 low-sodium chicken bouillon cubes

1. Set the Instant Pot to Saute and cook the ground beef with salt, pepper, garlic, and onion until the beef is no longer pink.

2. Pour in a small amount (about ½ cup) of tomato juice and scrape the bottom of the inner pot.

3. Press Cancel. Add all the remaining ingredients. Secure the lid and set the vent to sealing.

4. Manually set the cook time for 10 minutes on high pressure.

5. When the cooking time is over, let the pressure release naturally for 5 minutes, then manually release any remaining pressure. Serve and enjoy.

Protein: 14 g

Slow-Cooker Beef Stew

Becky Fixel, Grosse Pointe Farms, MI

Makes 8–10 servings
Prep. Time: 30 minutes ❧ *Cooking Time: 6 hours* ❧ *Ideal slow-cooker size: 3-qt.*

2 lb. chuck beef roast, cut into 1-inch pieces

¼ cup white rice flour

1½ tsp. kosher salt

½ tsp. black pepper

32 oz. low-sodium beef broth

1 onion, diced

1 tsp. Worcestershire sauce

1 bay leaf

1 tsp. paprika

4 carrots, sliced

3 potatoes, sliced thinly

1 celery rib, sliced

1. Place the meat in crock.

2. Mix the flour, salt, and pepper. Pour over the meat and mix well. Make sure to cover the meat with flour.

3. Add broth to the crock and stir well.

4. Add remaining ingredients and stir to mix well.

5. Cook on high for at least 5 hours, then on low for 1 hour. Remove bay leaf and serve.

Protein: 22 g

Colorful Beef Stew

Hope Comerford, Clinton Township, MI

Makes 6 servings
Prep. Time: 20 minutes   *Cooking Time: 8–9 hours*   *Ideal slow-cooker size: 4-qt.*

2 lb. boneless beef chuck roast, trimmed of fat and cut into ¾-inch pieces

1 large red onion, chopped

2 cups gluten-free low-sodium beef broth

6-oz. can low-sodium tomato paste

4 cloves garlic, minced

1 Tbsp. paprika

2 tsp. dried marjoram

½ tsp. black pepper

1 tsp. sea salt

1 red bell pepper, sliced

1 yellow bell pepper, sliced

1 orange bell pepper, sliced

1. Place all ingredients in the crock, except the sliced bell peppers, and stir.

2. Cover and cook on low for 8 to 9 hours. Stir in sliced bell peppers during the last 45 minutes of cooking time.

Protein: 32 g

Moroccan Spiced Stew

Melissa Paskvan, Novi, MI

Makes 6–8 servings

Prep. Time: 10 minutes ❧ Cooking Time: 8 hours ❧ Ideal slow-cooker size: 5-qt.

3 cups canned chopped tomatoes

3 cups gluten-free chicken stock

1 lb. lamb (ground or stew-cut pieces)

1 medium onion, chopped

⅛ tsp. fresh grated ginger

1½ tsp. cumin

¾ tsp. cinnamon

¾ tsp. turmeric

⅛–¼ tsp. cayenne pepper

½ cup shredded or chopped carrots

3 cups chopped sweet potato

Salt to taste

Pepper to taste

1. Place all ingredients in the crock and mix well to incorporate the spices.

2. Cover and cook on low for 8 hours.

Tip:

If you really want to seal in the warm spices, add 1 tablespoon olive oil to a pan and brown just the outsides of the lamb pieces and cook with onions and spices. Then add about 1 cup of the chicken stock to deglaze the pan and pour all ingredients from the pan to the slow cooker and add the remaining ingredients. This can also be made vegan using quinoa and chickpeas for the protein and substituting with vegetable stock. I add ½ cup rinsed quinoa to the recipe and 1 can garbanzo beans (chickpeas).

Serving suggestion:

Top with harissa for a zesty, warm flavor. Ladle this stew over brown rice or millet for a filling meal. Cook with ½ cup dried apricots or dates to impart a sweet taste.

Protein: 16 g

Beef and Black Bean Chili

Eileen B. Jarvis, St. Augustine, FL

Makes 8 servings
Prep. Time:10 minutes   *Cooking Time: 20 minutes*

I tsp. olive oil

I lb. 95% lean ground beef

I small onion, chopped

2 (15-oz.) cans no-salt-added black beans, rinsed and drained

¾ cup water or reduced-sodium beef stock

I cup medium or hot chunky salsa

16-oz. can no-salt-added tomato sauce

I Tbsp. chili powder

Low-fat sour cream, *optional*

Shredded reduced-fat cheddar cheese, *optional*

1. Set the Instant Pot to Saute and heat the oil in the inner pot.

2. Brown the beef until no longer pink along with the onion.

3. Press Cancel. Add the remaining ingredients except for the sour cream and shredded cheese, then secure the lid. Set the vent to sealing.

4. Set the Instant Pot to Chili/Beans and set the cook time for 20 minutes.

5. When the cooking time is over, release the pressure manually.

6. When serving, if you wish, top individual servings with sour cream and/or a sprinkle of shredded reduced-fat cheddar cheese.

Protein: 24 g

Meatless

White Bean Soup

Esther H. Becker, Gordonville, PA

Makes 6 servings

Prep. Time: 5 minutes   •   Soaking Time: Overnight (optional)   •   Cooking Time: 9 minutes

8 oz. (about 1¼ cups) dried white beans

4 cups water

3 cups low-fat, low-sodium vegetable stock

1 tsp. grapeseed or olive oil

1 onion, diced

2 cups raw sweet potatoes (about 2 medium potatoes), diced

1 cup green bell pepper, diced

¼ tsp. ground cloves

¼ tsp. black pepper

½ tsp. dried thyme

½ cup low-sugar ketchup

¼ cup molasses

¼ plus 2 Tbsp. nutritional yeast, *divided*

1. In a pot of water, soak the beans overnight. Drain and rinse. Place drained beans in the inner pot of the Instant Pot.

2. Pour in the water, vegetable stock, grapeseed oil, onion, sweet potatoes, bell pepper, ground cloves, black pepper, and thyme.

3. Secure the lid and set the vent to sealing.

4. Manually set the cook time to 9 minutes at high pressure.

5. When the cooking time is over, allow the pressure to release naturally. When the pin drops, remove the lid.

6. Stir in the ketchup and molasses. Add more water if you would like the soup to be thinner.

7. Sprinkle 1 tablespoon nutritional yeast on top of each serving.

Tips:

1. Adding the teaspoon of oil to the pot keeps foam from becoming too great in the pot and clogging the vent.

2. If you don't want to soak the beans, or forget to soak the beans, simply set the cook time to 31 minutes on high pressure.

Protein: 13 g

Cannellini Bean Soup

Hope Comerford, Clinton Township, MI

Makes 6–8 servings
Prep. Time: 10 minutes ❧ *Soaking Time: Overnight (optional)* ❧ *Cooking Time: 30 minutes*

2 Tbsp. extra-virgin olive oil

4 cloves garlic, sliced very thin

1 small onion, chopped

2 heads escarole, well washed and cut medium-fine (about 8 cups)

8-oz. bag dry cannellini beans, soaked overnight

8 cups low-sodium vegetable stock

3 basil leaves, chopped fine

¼ cup plus 2 Tbsp. Parmesan cheese shavings, *divided*

Tip:

If you don't have time to soak the beans overnight, simply cook the soup on high pressure for 51 minutes instead.

1. Set the Instant Pot to Saute and heat the olive oil.

2. Sauté the garlic, onion, and escarole until the onion is translucent.

3. Press Cancel and add the beans and vegetable stock.

4. Secure the lid and set the vent to sealing.

5. Manually set the time for 25 minutes on high pressure.

6. When the cooking time is over, let the pressure release naturally. Remove the lid when the pin drops and spoon into serving bowls.

7. Top each bowl with a sprinkle of the chopped basil leaves and 1 tablespoon Parmesan shavings

Protein: 8 g

Chipotle Navy Bean Soup

Rebecca Weybright, Manheim, PA

Makes 6 servings
Prep. Time: 10 minutes   Cooking Time: 8 hours
Standing Time: 12 hours   Ideal slow-cooker size: 5-qt.

1½ cups dried navy beans,
soaked overnight

1 onion, chopped

1 dried chipotle chili,
soaked 10–15 minutes in cold water

4 cups water

1–2 tsp. salt

2 cups canned tomatoes with juice

1. Drain soaked beans.

2. Add to slow cooker with onion, chili, and water.

3. Cover and cook on low for 8 hours until beans are creamy.

4. Add salt and tomatoes.

5. Use an immersion blender to puree soup.

Protein: 12 g

Brown Lentil Soup

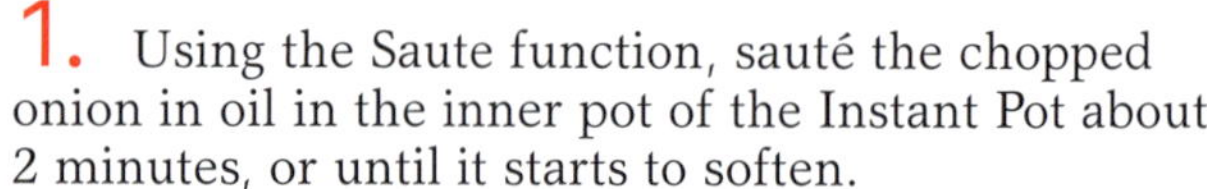

Colleen Heatwole, Burton, MI

Makes 3–5 servings
Prep. Time: 15 minutes   *Cooking Time: 20 minutes*

1 medium onion, chopped

1 Tbsp. olive oil

1 medium carrot, diced

2 cloves garlic, minced

1 small bay leaf

1 lb. brown lentils

5 cups vegetable broth

1 tsp. salt

¼ tsp. ground black pepper

½ tsp. lemon juice

1. Using the Saute function, sauté the chopped onion in oil in the inner pot of the Instant Pot about 2 minutes, or until it starts to soften.

2. Add diced carrot and sauté 3 minutes more until it begins to soften. Stir frequently or it will stick.

3. Add garlic and sauté 1 more minute.

4. Add bay leaf, lentils, and broth to pot.

5. Secure the lid and make sure vent is at sealing. Using Manual setting, select 14 minutes and cook on high pressure.

6. When cooking time is up, do a quick release of the pressure.

7. Discard bay leaf.

8. Stir in salt, pepper, and lemon juice, then adjust seasonings to taste.

Protein: 8 g

Lentil Spinach Soup

Marilyn Widrick, Adams, NY

Makes 4–6 servings
Prep. Time: 10 minutes & *Cooking Time: 2½ hours* & *Ideal slow-cooker size: 5-qt.*

1 Tbsp. olive oil
4 medium carrots, chopped
1 small onion, diced
1 tsp. ground cumin
14½-oz. can diced tomatoes
14½-oz. can gluten-free vegetable broth
1 cup dry lentils
2 cups water
¼ tsp. salt
⅛ tsp. pepper
5-oz. bag fresh spinach, chopped
¾ cup shredded Parmesan cheese
½ cup Greek yogurt

1. Heat 1 tablespoon olive oil in cooking pot. Add carrots and onion. Cook 8 to 10 minutes over medium heat.

2. Place carrots and onions in slow cooker. Add cumin, diced tomatoes, vegetable broth, dry lentils, water, salt, and pepper.

3. Cover and cook on low 2 hours.

4. Add spinach. Cook on low an additional 15 to 25 minutes.

5. Serve each bowl with a bit of shredded Parmesan cheese and a dollop of Greek yogurt.

Protein: 22 g

Vegetarian Split Pea Soup

Colleen Heatwole, Burton, MI

Makes 6 servings

Prep. Time: 30 minutes ❧ *Cooking Time: 5–6 hours* ❧ *Ideal slow-cooker size: 6-qt.*

1 lb. split peas, sorted and rinsed

2 quarts gluten-free low-sodium vegetable broth

2 cups water

1 large onion, chopped

2 cloves garlic, minced

3 celery ribs, chopped

3 medium carrots, chopped finely

2 bay leaves

1 tsp. kosher salt

1 tsp. black pepper

1. Combine all ingredients and add to slow cooker.

2. Cover and cook on low for 5 to 6 hours. Remove bay leaves and serve.

Serving suggestion:

If creamy texture is desired, blend with immersion blender

Tip:

If desired, add more salt after cooking, but note that this will increase sodium content.

Protein: 19 g

Tempehtilla Soup

Hope Comerford, Clinton Township, MI

Makes 6–8 servings

Prep. Time: 10 minutes ❧ Cooking Time: 6 hours ❧ Ideal slow-cooker size: 5-qt.

3 large tomatoes, chopped

1 cup chopped red onion

1 jalapeño, seeded and minced

2 tsp. cumin

2 tsp. chili powder

2 tsp. onion powder

2 tsp. garlic powder

2 tsp. lime juice

8 cups vegan vegetable broth

2 (8-oz.) blocks tempeh, cut into thin strips

Optional Garnishes

Fresh chopped cilantro

Avocado slices

Vegan mozzarella cheese

1. Add the tomatoes, onion, and jalapeño to the crock.

2. Add all the seasonings and lime juice and pour in the vegetable broth.

3. Place the tempeh strips on top.

4. Cover and cook on low for 6 hours.

5. If desired, serve each bowl of soup with fresh chopped cilantro, avocado slices, and freshly grated vegan mozzarella cheese.

Tip:

If you don't have time for freshly chopped tomatoes, use a can of diced or chopped tomatoes.

Protein: 12 g

"Meatball" Pasta Soup

Michele Ruvola, Vestal, NY

Makes 4–5 servings
Prep. Time: 10 minutes & *Cooking Time: 9 minutes*

1 cup diced carrots

½ cup diced celery

¾ cup diced onion

12.7-oz. bag frozen meatless meatballs

1 ½ cups protein pasta
(shape of your choice)

40 oz. vegetable broth

1 tsp. salt

½ tsp. black pepper

2 Tbsp. diced parsley

2 Tbsp. diced green onions

1. Place all ingredients, except the parsley and green onions, in the inner pot of the Instant Pot and stir.

2. Secure the lid, make sure vent is set to sealing, then put on Manual function, set to high pressure, for 9 minutes.

3. Use quick release to release pressure, then stir.

4. Top with parsley and green onions.

Protein: 21 g

Pumpkin Chili

Hope Comerford, Clinton Township, MI

Makes 8 servings

Prep. Time: 10 minutes   Cooking Time: 7–8 hours   Ideal slow-cooker size: 6-qt.

16-oz. can kidney beans, rinsed and drained

16-oz. can black beans, rinsed and drained

1 large onion, chopped

½ green pepper, chopped

1 lb. ground turkey, browned

15-oz. can pumpkin puree

4 cups fresh chopped tomatoes

3 Tbsp. garlic powder

1 Tbsp. ancho chili powder

1 tsp. salt

2 tsp. cumin

¼ tsp. pepper

4 Tbsp. gluten-free beef bouillon granules

5 cups water

1. Place the kidney beans, black beans, onion, and pepper in the crock.

2. Crumble the ground turkey over the top and spoon the pumpkin puree on top of that.

3. Add the remaining ingredients and stir.

4. Cover and cook on low for 7 to 8 hours.

Serving suggestion:

Garnish with toasted pepitas.

Protein: 26 g

Main Dishes

Chicken

Rotisserie Chicken

Hope Comerford, Clinton Township, MI

Makes 4 servings
Prep. Time: 5 minutes ❧ Cooking Time: 33 minutes

3-lb. whole chicken

2 Tbsp. olive oil, *divided*

Salt to taste

Pepper to taste

10 cloves fresh garlic, peeled and left whole

1 cup low-sodium chicken stock, broth, or water

2 Tbsp. garlic powder

2 tsp. onion powder

½ tsp. basil

½ tsp. cumin

½ tsp. chili powder

Serving suggestion:

Serve with Artichokes and Brown Rice (page 195), Beans 'n Greens (page 188), or Cauliflower Cassoulet (page 203).

1. Rub the chicken with 1 tablespoon olive oil and sprinkle with salt and pepper.

2. Place the garlic cloves inside the chicken. Use butcher's twine to secure the legs.

3. Press the Saute button on the Instant Pot, then add the rest of the olive oil to the inner pot.

4. When the pot is hot, place the chicken inside. You are just trying to sear it, so leave it for about 4 minutes on each side.

5. Remove the chicken and set aside. Place the trivet at the bottom of the inner pot and pour in the chicken stock.

6. Mix together the remaining seasonings and rub them all over the entire chicken.

7. Place the chicken back inside the inner pot, breast-side up, on top of the trivet and secure the lid to the sealing position.

8. Manually set the cook time for 25 minutes on high pressure.

9. When cook time is up, allow the pressure to release naturally for 15 minutes, then manually release any remaining pressure.

10. Let the chicken rest for 5 to 10 minutes before serving.

Protein: 67 g

Main Dishes: Chicken   ❧   **99**

Chicken Dinner in a Packet

Bonnie Whaling, Clearfield, PA

Makes 4 servings
Prep. Time: 10 minutes   &   Cooking Time: 15 minutes

I cup water

4 (5-oz.) boneless, skinless chicken breast halves

2 cups sliced fresh mushrooms

2 medium carrots, cut in thin strips, about I cup

I medium zucchini, unpeeled and sliced, about I ½ cups

2 Tbsp. olive oil or canola oil

2 Tbsp. lemon juice

I Tbsp. fresh basil or I tsp. dry basil

¼ tsp. salt

¼ tsp. black pepper

1. Pour the water into the inner pot of the Instant Pot and place the trivet or a steamer basket on top.

2. Fold four 12-inch × 28-inch pieces of foil in half to make four 12-inch × 14-inch rectangles. Place one chicken breast half on each piece of foil.

3. Top with the mushrooms, carrots, and zucchini, dividing the vegetables equally between the chicken bundles.

4. In a small bowl, stir together the oil, lemon juice, basil, salt, and pepper.

5. Drizzle the oil mixture over the vegetables and chicken.

6. Pull up two opposite edges of foil. Seal with a double fold. Then fold in the remaining edges, leaving enough space for steam to build.

7. Place the bundles on top of the trivet, or inside the steamer basket.

8. Secure the lid and set the vent to sealing.

9. Manually set the cook time for 15 minutes at high pressure.

10. When the cooking time is over, let the pressure release naturally. When the pin drops, remove the lid.

11. Serve dinners in foil packets, or transfer to serving plate.

Protein: 35 g

Italian Crockpot Chicken

Andrea Maher, West Chester, PA

Makes 6 servings

Prep. Time: 5 minutes ❧ *Cooking Time: 6–8 hours* ❧ *Ideal slow-cooker size: 6-qt.*

24 oz. boneless, skinless chicken breast, cut into small pieces

3 cups garbanzo beans

16-oz. bag frozen spinach

2 cups mushrooms

2 Tbsp. Mrs. Dash Italian seasoning

1 cup low-sodium gluten-free chicken broth

1. Add all ingredients to the slow cooker.

2. Cover and cook on low for 6 to 8 hours or high for 3 to 4 hours.

Serving suggestion:

Serve with Mushroom Risotto (page 193).

Protein: 36 g

Italian Chicken and Broccoli

Liz Clapper, Lancaster, PA

Makes 6 servings
Prep. Time: 15 minutes 🍳 Cooking Time: 5 minutes

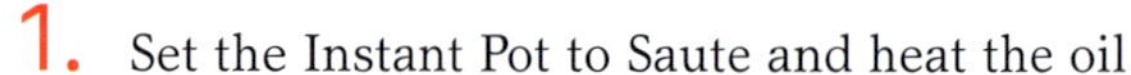

1 Tbsp. olive oil

1 head broccoli, chopped into florets (about 4 cups)

2 cloves garlic, finely chopped

1 lb. chicken tenderloins

4 medium carrots, sliced thin

2 cups uncooked whole-grain macaroni pasta

3 cups low-fat, low-sodium chicken broth

1½ Tbsp. Italian seasoning

¼ cup shredded reduced-fat Parmesan cheese

1. Set the Instant Pot to Saute and heat the oil.

2. Sauté the broccoli for 5 minutes in the inner pot. Set it aside in a bowl and cover to keep warm.

3. Add the garlic and chicken and sauté for 8 minutes.

4. Press Cancel. Add the carrots and stir. Pour the macaroni evenly over the top. Pour in the broth and Italian seasoning. Do not stir.

5. Secure the lid and set the vent to sealing.

6. Manually set the cook time for 5 minutes on high pressure.

7. When the cooking time is over, let the pressure release naturally for 5 minutes, then manually release the remaining pressure.

8. When the pin drops, remove the lid, sprinkle the contents with Parmesan, and serve immediately.

Serving suggestion:

Serve with White Beans with Sun-Dried Tomatoes (page 189).

Protein: 32 g

Garlic Mushroom Thighs

Elaine Vigoda, Rochester, NY

Makes 6 servings
Prep. Time: 15 minutes   Cooking Time: 4 hours   Ideal slow-cooker size: 5-qt.

3 Tbsp. gluten-free flour

6 boneless, skinless chicken thighs

8–10 cloves garlic, peeled and very lightly crushed

I Tbsp. olive oil

¾ lb. fresh mushrooms, any combination of varieties, cut into bite-size pieces

⅓ cup balsamic vinegar

1¼ cups gluten-free chicken broth or stock

1–2 bay leaves

½ tsp. dried thyme or 4 sprigs fresh thyme

2 tsp. apricot preserves (low-sugar or no-sugar-added preferred)

Serving suggestion:

Serve with cooked quinoa or alongside Perfect Pinto Beans (page 192).

1. Grease interior of slow cooker.

2. Place gluten-free flour in a strong plastic bag without any holes. Once by one, put each thigh in bag, hold the bag shut, and shake it to flour the thigh fully.

3. Place thighs in the crock. If you need to make a second layer, stagger the pieces so they don't directly overlap.

4. If you have time, sauté the garlic in oil in skillet just until it begins to brown. Otherwise, use raw.

5. Sprinkle garlic over thighs, including those on bottom layer.

6. Scatter cut-up mushrooms over thighs too, remembering those on the bottom layer.

7. Mix remaining ingredients together in a bowl, stirring to break up the preserves.

8. When well mixed, pour into the cooker along the edges so you don't wash the vegetables off the chicken pieces.

9. Cover and cook on low for 4 hours, or until an instant-read thermometer registers 160°F to 165°F when stuck into the thighs.

10. Serve meat topped with vegetables with sauce spooned over.

Protein: 24 g

Chicken Dijon Dinner

Barbara Stutzman, Crossville, TN

Makes 4–6 servings
Prep. Time: 20 minutes ❧ Cooking Time: 4 hours ❧ Ideal slow-cooker size: 6-qt.

2 lb. boneless, skinless chicken thighs

2 cloves garlic, minced

1 Tbsp. olive oil

6 Tbsp. white wine vinegar

4 Tbsp. reduced-sodium soy sauce
or Bragg Liquid Aminos

4 Tbsp. Dijon mustard

1 lb. sliced mushrooms

1. Grease slow-cooker crock.

2. Place thighs in the crock. If you need to add a second layer, stagger the pieces so they don't directly overlap each other.

3. Stir together garlic, oil, vinegar, soy sauce, and mustard until well mixed.

4. Gently stir in mushrooms.

5. Spoon sauce into crock, making sure to cover all thighs with some of the sauce.

6. Cover and cook on low for 4 hours, or until instant-read thermometer registers 160°F when stuck in center of chicken.

7. Serve chicken topped with sauce.

Serving suggestion:

Serve with Mushroom Risotto (page 193).

Protein: 30 g

Chicken Mole

Bernadette Veenstra, Grand Rapids, MI

Makes 8 servings
Prep. Time: 30 minutes   Cooking Time: 4–5 hours   Ideal slow-cooker size: 6-qt.

1 Tbsp. olive oil

8–10 chicken thighs, skinned and lightly salted and peppered

1 large onion

4–6 cloves garlic, minced

4 tsp. chili powder

4 tsp. unsweetened cocoa powder

¼ tsp. cinnamon

2½ cups low-sodium chicken broth or stock

2 Tbsp. natural creamy peanut butter

2 Tbsp. no-salt-added tomato paste

4 cups cooked brown rice

½ cup dark raisins

½ cup loosely packed cilantro leaves

Lime wedges

1. Heat olive oil in a large skillet. In several batches, brown all sides of chicken (about 10 minutes total).

2. Place chicken in bottom of slow cooker lightly coated with cooking spray. Discard all but 1 tablespoon of pan drippings.

3. Heat pan drippings or oil in same skillet. Add onion and cook, stirring until softened (about 5 minutes). Add garlic, chili powder, cocoa powder, and cinnamon to skillet and cook, stirring 1 minute.

4. Stir in broth, peanut butter, and tomato paste.

5. Pour sauce over chicken in slow cooker.

6. Cook on low for 4 to 5 hours, or until chicken registers 165°F on meat thermometer.

7. Serve over cooked brown rice and garnish with raisins, cilantro, and lime wedges.

Protein: 15 g

Honey Balsamic Chicken

Hope Comerford, Clinton Township, MI

Makes 4–6 servings
Prep. Time: 5 minutes   Cooking Time: 7–8 hours   Ideal slow-cooker size: 5- or 6-qt.

4 cups chopped red potatoes

1½ tsp. kosher salt, *divided*

1 tsp. pepper, *divided*

8–10 boneless, skinless chicken thighs

1 cup sliced red onion

1 pint cherry tomatoes

½ cup balsamic vinegar

¼ cup honey

2 Tbsp. olive oil

¼ tsp. red pepper flakes

½ tsp. dried thyme

½ tsp. dried rosemary

3 cloves garlic, minced

3 cups green beans

1. Spray crock with nonstick cooking spray.

2. Place potatoes in bottom of crock. Sprinkle with ½ teaspoon of salt and ½ teaspoon of pepper.

3. Place chicken on top of potatoes and place onions and cherry tomatoes over the top.

4. Mix together the balsamic vinegar, honey, olive oil, 1 teaspoon salt, remaining ½ teaspoon pepper, red pepper flakes, thyme, rosemary, and garlic. Pour this mixture over the chicken, tomatoes, and potatoes.

5. Cook on low for 7 to 8 hours, or until potatoes are tender.

6. Add the green beans on top 20 to 30 minutes before serving.

Serving suggestions:

To serve, spoon the juices from the crock over the chicken and vegetables. Serve with Herbed Rice Pilaf (page 196).

Protein: 19 g

Juicy Orange Chicken

Andrea Maher, West Chester, PA

Makes 6 servings
Prep. Time: 10 minutes   Cooking Time: 6–8 hours   Ideal slow-cooker size: 5- or 6-qt.

18–24 oz. boneless, skinless chicken breast, cut into small pieces

1 cup orange juice, no additives

¼ cup honey

6 small oranges, peeled and sliced

¼ cup Bragg Liquid Aminos

6 cups broccoli slaw

1. Add all the ingredients to the slow cooker except the broccoli slaw.

2. Cover and cook on high for 3 to 4 hours or on low for 6 to 8 hours.

3. Divide mixture between 6 mason jars.

4. Add 1 cup broccoli slaw to each mason jar.

5. Pour into a bowl when you're ready to eat!

Tip:

For extra protein, serve over cooked quinoa.

Protein: 30 g

Asian-Style Chicken with Pineapple

Andrea Maher, West Chester, PA

Makes 6 servings
Prep. Time: 10 minutes ❧ *Cooking Time: 3–8 hours* ❧ *Ideal slow-cooker size: 5- or 6-qt.*

24 oz. boneless, skinless chicken breast cut into bite-size pieces

3 cups pineapple, cubed

¼ cup Bragg Liquid Aminos

1 Tbsp. brown sugar

½ cup chopped onion or 2 Tbsp. onion powder

1 cup low-sodium gluten-free chicken broth or stock

½ tsp. ground ginger

2 (16-oz.) bags frozen Szechuan mixed veggies or any mixed veggies

1. Add all ingredients except for frozen veggies to the slow cooker.

2. Cover and cook on high 3 to 4 hours or low 6 to 8 hours.

3. Add frozen veggies in the last 1 to 2 hours.

Serving suggestion:

Serve with Quinoa with Almonds and Cranberries (page 201).

Protein: 32 g

Thai Chicken Rice Bowls

Vonnie Oyer, Hubbard, OR

Makes 4–6 servings
Prep. Time: 15 minutes ⚖ Cooking Time: 20 minutes

2 Tbsp. olive oil

2 lb. chicken breasts (about 4)

½ cup sweet chili Thai sauce

3 Tbsp. soy sauce

½ Tbsp. fish sauce

½ Tbsp. minced ginger

½ Tbsp. minced garlic

1 tsp. lime juice

1 tsp. sriracha

1 Tbsp. peanut butter

1 cup uncooked long-grain brown rice

2 cups broth

Optional Garnishes

Cilantro

Shredded carrots

Peanuts

1. Select Saute on the Instant Pot and add the olive oil to the inner pot.

2. Sear the chicken for 2 to 3 minutes on both sides to seal in their juices. Remove to a glass baking dish and turn off the Instant Pot.

3. Mix the sweet chili Thai sauce, soy sauce, fish sauce, ginger, garlic, lime juice, sriracha, and peanut butter together.

4. Pour the sauce over the chicken breasts in glass dish.

5. Place the rice in the inner pot of the Instant Pot and add the chicken and sauce over top.

6. Add the broth and secure the lid. Make sure vent is on sealing.

7. Select Manual (on high pressure) and set the timer to 10 minutes. Let pressure release naturally.

8. Take out and shred the chicken with two forks. Mix the chicken back in with the rice.

9. Garnish with cilantro, shredded carrots, and peanuts, if desired.

Protein: 40 g

Chicken with Spiced Sesame Sauce

Colleen Heatwole, Burton, MI

Makes 4–6 servings
Prep. Time: 20 minutes   Cooking Time: 8 minutes

2 Tbsp. tahini (sesame sauce)

½ cup water

1 Tbsp. soy sauce

¼ cup chopped onion

1 tsp. red wine vinegar

2 tsp. minced garlic

1 tsp. shredded ginger root (Microplane works best)

2 lb. chicken breast, chopped into 8 portions

1. Place first seven ingredients in bottom of the inner pot of the Instant Pot.

2. Add coarsely chopped chicken on top.

3. Secure the lid and make sure vent is at sealing. Set for 8 minutes using Manual setting. When cook time is up, let the pressure release naturally for 10 minutes, then perform a quick release.

4. Remove ingredients and shred chicken with forks. Combine with other ingredients in pot for a tasty sandwich filling or sauce.

Serving suggestion:

Serve on Ezekial bread or over cooked quinoa.

Protein: 35 g

Southwestern Shredded Chicken

Hope Comerford, Clinton Township, MI

Makes 4 servings
Prep. Time: 8–10 minutes   Cooking Time: 5–6 hours   Ideal slow-cooker size: 3-qt.

1½ lb. boneless, skinless chicken breast

1 Tbsp. chili powder

2 tsp. garlic powder

1 tsp. cumin

1 tsp. onion powder

½ tsp. kosher salt

¼ tsp. pepper

1 medium onion, chopped

14.5-oz. can diced tomatoes

4-oz. can diced green chilies

½ cup nonfat Greek yogurt

Optional Toppings

Lettuce

Shredded cheese

Greek yogurt

Salsa

1. Place the chicken in the slow cooker.

2. Mix together the chili powder, garlic powder, cumin, onion powder, kosher salt, and pepper. Sprinkle this over both sides of the chicken.

3. Sprinkle the onion over the top of the chicken and pour the can of diced tomatoes and the can of green chilies over the top.

4. Cover and cook on low for 5 to 6 hours.

5. Turn the slow cooker to warm. Remove the chicken and shred it between two forks.

6. Slowly whisk in the nonfat Greek yogurt with the juices in the crock. Replace the chicken in the crock and stir to mix in the juices.

Serving suggestion:

Serve this over brown rice or quinoa topped with some shredded lettuce, shredded cheese, and fresh salsa.

Protein: 43 g

Easy Enchilada Shredded Chicken

Hope Comerford, Clinton Township, MI

Makes 10–14 servings

Prep. Time: 5 minutes ⚹ *Cooking Time: 5–6 hours* ⚹ *Ideal slow-cooker size: 3- or 5-qt.*

5–6 lb. boneless, skinless chicken breast

14.5-oz. can petite diced tomatoes

1 medium onion, chopped

8 oz. red enchilada sauce

½ tsp. salt

½ tsp. chili powder

½ tsp. basil

½ tsp. garlic powder

¼ tsp. pepper

1. Place chicken in the crock.

2. Add the remaining ingredients.

3. Cover and cook on low for 5 to 6 hours.

4. Remove chicken and shred it between two forks. Place the shredded chicken back in the crock and stir to mix in the juices.

Serving suggestion:

Serve over salad, brown rice, quinoa, sweet potatoes, nachos, or corn tortillas. Add a dollop of yogurt and a sprinkle of fresh cilantro.

Protein: 42 g

Skinny Chicken Stroganoff

Carol Sherwood, Batavia, NY

Makes 6 servings
Prep. Time: 10 minutes   Cooking Time: 5 minutes

1 tsp. olive oil

1 cup chopped onion

1 clove garlic, pressed

1½ lb. boneless, skinless chicken breasts, cut into bite-size pieces

⅛ tsp. black pepper

8 oz. uncooked whole wheat wide egg noodles

8 oz. sliced fresh mushrooms

1 cup low-fat low-sodium chicken broth

¾ cup reduced-fat sour cream

4 slices turkey bacon, cooked and broken, *optional*

2 Tbsp. chopped fresh parsley, *optional*

2 Tbsp. cornstarch

2 Tbsp. cold water

1. Set the Instant Pot to Saute and heat the olive oil in the inner pot.

2. Sauté the onion and garlic for 3 minutes. Press Cancel.

3. Add the chicken and pepper. Stir to coat everything in the pot. Pour the noodles on top of the chicken mixture. Evenly spread out. Evenly spread the mushrooms on top of the noodles.

4. Pour the chicken broth on top. Secure the lid and set the vent to sealing.

5. Manually set the cook time for 2 minutes at high pressure.

6. When the cooking time is over, let the pressure release naturally for 10 minutes, then manually release the remaining pressure.

7. When the pin drops, remove the lid. Stir.

8. Remove about ¼ cup of the liquid from the inner pot, and, in a separate bowl, mix this with the sour cream, tempering it. Slowly add this tempered sour cream to the inner pot, stirring constantly. Stir in the bacon and parsley if desired.

9. Set the Instant Pot to Saute. In a small bowl, whisk together the cornstarch and water. Add this to the inner pot and stir. Cook for a couple of minutes, or until thickened to your liking, then press Cancel.

Protein: 49 g

Spiced Lentils with Chicken and Rice

Janelle Reitz, Lancaster, PA

Makes 6 servings
Prep. Time: 10 minutes & Cooking Time: 15 minutes

I Tbsp. olive oil

3-inch cinnamon stick

¾ tsp. ground cumin

6 cloves garlic, minced

I onion, sliced

¾ lb. boneless, skinless chicken breast, cubed

I cup uncooked brown rice, rinsed

½ cup brown lentils, rinsed

I tsp. ground cardamom

2½ cups low-sodium, fat-free chicken broth

½ cup raisins

2 Tbsp. chopped fresh cilantro

½ cup toasted almonds, *optional*

1. Set the Instant Pot to Saute and heat the oil.

2. Sauté the cinnamon stick, cumin, and garlic for 2 minutes.

3. Add the onion and sauté until tender, about 3 to 5 minutes.

4. Press Cancel. Add the chicken, brown rice, lentils, and cardamom, in that order. Pour in the chicken broth. Do not stir.

5. Secure the lid and set the vent to sealing.

6. Manually set the cook time for 15 minutes on high pressure.

7. When the cooking time is over, let the pressure release naturally for 15 minutes, then manually release the remaining pressure.

8. When the pin drops, remove the lid. Remove the cinnamon stick. Add the raisins, cilantro, and almonds (if using).

Protein: 25 g

Buffalo Chicken Meatballs

Hope Comerford, Clinton Township, MI

Makes 6 servings
Prep. Time: 20–30 minutes & Cooking Time: 6 hours & Ideal slow-cooker size: 5- or 6-qt.

1½ lb. ground chicken

¾ cup gluten-free hot sauce of your choice, *divided*

2 Tbsp. dry minced onion

2 Tbsp. garlic powder

¼ tsp. pepper

1 egg

1 cup gluten-free panko breadcrumbs

1½–2 Tbsp. coconut oil

2 tsp. gluten-free low-sodium chicken bouillon granules

1 cup water

2 cups nonfat plain Greek yogurt

2 Tbsp. cornstarch

Serving suggestions:

Serve meatballs over brown rice or quinoa with a fresh salad on the side. If desired, add more hot sauce to taste.

1. In a bowl, combine the ground chicken, ½ cup hot sauce, minced onion, garlic powder, pepper, egg, and gluten-free panko breadcrumbs.

2. Heat the coconut oil in a large skillet over medium-high heat.

3. Roll the chicken mixture into 1½- to 2-inch balls. Place them in the skillet, turning them regularly so they're seared on each side.

4. Place the seared meatballs into the crock. Sprinkle them with the chicken bouillon granules and pour in the water.

5. Cover and cook on low for 6 hours.

6. Remove the meatballs in a covered dish to keep them warm.

7. In a bowl, stir together the Greek yogurt, cornstarch, and remaining ¼ cup of hot sauce. Gently whisk this back into the crock with the juices.

8. You can either place the browned meatballs back into the sauce to coat them or serve the meatballs with the sauce spooned over the top.

Protein: 30 g

Turkey

Thyme and Garlic Turkey Breast

Hope Comerford, Clinton Township, MI

Makes 6–8 servings
Prep. Time: 10 minutes   ☙   Cooking Time: 7–8 hours   ☙   Ideal slow-cooker size: 6- or 7-qt.

4 lb. bone-in turkey breast, giblets removed if there are any, skin removed, washed and patted dry

¼ cup olive oil

1 Tbsp. balsamic vinegar

1 Tbsp. water

1 orange, juiced

6 cloves garlic, minced

1½ tsp. dried thyme

1 tsp. onion powder

1 tsp. kosher salt

1. Place turkey breast in crock.

2. Mix together the remaining ingredients and pour over the turkey breast. Rub it in on all sides with clean hands.

3. Cover and cook on low for 7 to 8 hours.

Serving suggestion:

Serve with Herbed Rice Pilaf (page 196), Mushroom Risotto (page 193), and Cauliflower Cassoulet (page 203).

Protein: 50 g

Turkey with Mushroom Sauce

Judi Manos, West Islip, NY

Makes 12 servings
Prep. Time: 25 minutes ⚬ *Cooking Time: 7–8 hours* ⚬ *Ideal slow-cooker size: 6-qt.*

1 large boneless, skinless turkey breast, halved

2 Tbsp. melted coconut oil

2 Tbsp. dried parsley

½ tsp. dried oregano

½ tsp. kosher salt

¼ tsp. black pepper

½ cup white wine

1 cup fresh mushrooms, sliced

2 Tbsp. cornstarch

¼ cup cold water

Serving suggestion:

Serve with Moroccan Sweet Potato Medley (page 187).

1. Place turkey in slow cooker. Brush with coconut oil.

2. Mix together parsley, oregano, salt, pepper, and wine. Pour over turkey.

3. Top with mushrooms.

4. Cover and cook on low for 7 to 8 hours or just until turkey is tender.

5. Remove turkey and keep warm.

6. Skim any fat from cooking juices.

7. In a saucepan over low heat, combine cornstarch and water and mix until smooth. Gradually add cooking juices from the crock. Bring to a boil. Cook and stir 2 minutes until thickened.

8. Slice turkey and serve with sauce.

Protein: 9 g

Daddy's Pasta Fasool

Maria Shevlin, Sicklerville, NJ

Makes 8 servings
Prep. Time: 15 minutes   Cooking Time: 6 minutes

1 cup tomato sauce

1 cup diced onion

½ cup diced carrots

½ cup diced celery

1 Tbsp. chopped fresh celery leaves

14½-oz. can petite diced tomatoes

1 cup precooked ground turkey

3–4 cloves garlic, minced

1 bay leaf

½ tsp. onion powder

½ tsp. garlic powder

¼ tsp. basil

¼ tsp. oregano

½ tsp. parsley flakes

½ tsp. salt

¼ tsp. black pepper

15½-oz. can cannellini beans, rinsed and drained (I use Goya brand)

1 cup elbows or similar small protein pasta of your choice

4 cups chicken bone broth

1. In the inner pot of the Instant Pot, add the sauce, onion, carrots, celery, celery leaf, tomatoes, turkey, garlic, and seasonings, and stir.

2. Set to Saute for 5 minutes, stirring occasionally.

3. After 5 minutes add the beans, pasta, and bone broth, in that order.

4. Lock lid, set vent to sealing, then set on Manual at high pressure for 6 minutes.

5. Release the pressure manually when cooking time is over.

Protein: 13 g

Turkey "Spaghetti" Quinoa

Hope Comerford, Clinton Township, MI

Makes 8–10 servings
Prep. Time: 10–15 minutes ❧ Cooking Time: 5 hours ❧ Ideal slow-cooker size: 5- or 6-qt.

2 lb. lean ground turkey

½ tsp. salt

⅛ tsp. pepper

1 tsp. garlic powder

1 tsp. onion powder

1 cup quinoa

1 cup chopped onion

1 cup shredded mozzarella cheese (for dairy-free, substitute dairy-free cheese or leave out)

4 cups tomato sauce

2 cups water

1. Brown turkey with the salt, pepper, garlic powder, and onion powder.

2. Spray crock with nonstick cooking spray.

3. Place ground turkey in bottom of crock. Top with quinoa, onion, and shredded mozzarella.

4. Pour tomato sauce and water into crock. Stir so everything is mixed.

5. Cover and cook on low for 5 hours.

Protein: 31 g

Turkey Meatloaf

Delores A. Gnagey, Saginaw, MI

Makes 4–5 servings
Prep. Time: 15 minutes   Cooking Time: 15 minutes   Standing Time: 10 minutes

1 cup plus 1 Tbsp. water, *divided*

1 lb. lean ground turkey

½ small onion, minced

1½ Tbsp. minced fresh parsley

2 egg whites

2 Tbsp. skim milk

½ tsp. dry mustard

¼ tsp. salt

⅛ tsp. ground white pepper

Pinch nutmeg

1 slice Ezekial bread, lightly toasted, made into coarse crumbs

1 Tbsp. low-sugar ketchup

Serving suggestion:

Serve with Moroccan Sweet Potato Medley (page 187).

Protein: 24 g

1. Set the trivet inside the inner pot of the Instant Pot and pour in 1 cup water.

2. In a medium bowl, mix the ground turkey, onion, and parsley. Set aside.

3. In another bowl, whisk the egg whites. Add the milk, mustard, salt, pepper, and nutmeg to the egg. Whisk to blend.

4. Add the breadcrumbs to the egg mixture. Let rest 10 minutes.

5. Add the egg mixture to the meat mixture and blend well.

6. Spray the inside of a 7-inch springform baking pan, then spread the meat mixture into it.

7. Blend together the ketchup and 1 tablespoon water in a small bowl. Spread the mixture on top of the meat. Cover the pan with aluminum foil.

8. Place the springform pan on top of the trivet inside the inner pot.

9. Secure the lid and set the vent to sealing.

10. Manually set the cook time for 15 minutes on high pressure.

11. When the cooking time is over, let the pressure release naturally.

12. When the pin drops, remove the lid and use oven mitts to carefully remove the trivet from the inner pot.

13. Allow the meat to stand 10 minutes before slicing to serve.

Healthy Joes

Gladys M. High, Ephrata, PA

Makes 4–5 servings
Prep. Time: 15 minutes   Cooking Time: 10 minutes

1 Tbsp. olive oil

1 cup chopped onion

2 cloves garlic, chopped

1 medium bell pepper, chopped

1 medium zucchini, shredded, *optional*

1 lb. ground turkey sausage

1½ cups no-salt-added diced tomatoes

1 Tbsp. chili powder

1 tsp. paprika

Black pepper to taste

½ cup water

¾ cup no-salt-added tomato sauce

1 Tbsp. no-salt-added tomato paste

1½ Tbsp. brown sugar

4–5 whole wheat hamburger buns

1. Set the Instant Pot to Saute and heat the oil in the inner pot.

2. Sauté the onion and garlic for about 3 minutes. Add the bell pepper and zucchini (if using) and continue to sauté for about 5 minutes.

3. Add the turkey sausage to the inner pot and continue to cook for about 4 minutes. Press Cancel.

4. Pour in the tomatoes, chili powder, paprika, black pepper, water, tomato sauce, tomato paste, and brown sugar. Stir to combine all ingredients.

5. Secure the lid and set the vent to sealing.

6. Manually set the cook time for 10 minutes at high pressure.

7. When the cooking time is over, let the pressure release naturally for 5 minutes, then manually release the remaining pressure.

8. When the pin drops, remove the lid, stir. Spoon the mixture into the buns and enjoy.

Protein: 28 g

Pork

Savory Pork Roast

Mary Louise Martin, Boyd, WI

Makes 4–6 servings

Prep. Time: 15 minutes ❧ *Cooking Time: 3½–4½ hours* ❧ *Ideal slow-cooker size: oval 6-qt.*

4-lb. boneless pork butt roast

1 tsp. ground ginger

1 Tbsp. fresh minced rosemary

½ tsp. mace or nutmeg

1 tsp. coarsely ground black pepper

2 tsp. salt

2 cups water

1. Grease interior of slow-cooker crock.

2. Place roast in slow cooker.

3. In a bowl, mix spices and seasonings together. Sprinkle half on top of roast, pushing down on spices to encourage them to stick.

4. Flip roast and sprinkle with rest of spices, again, pushing down to make them stick.

5. Pour 2 cups water around the edge, being careful not to wash spices off meat.

6. Cover. Cook on low 3½–4½ hours, or until instant-read meat thermometer registers 140°F when stuck into center of roast.

Serving suggestion:

Serve with Quinoa with Almonds and Cranberries (page 201).

Protein: 52 g

Salsa Verde Pork

Hope Comerford, Clinton Township, MI

Makes 6 servings
Prep. Time: 20 minutes   &   Cooking Time: 6–6½ hours   &   Ideal slow-cooker size: 4-qt.

1½ lb.-boneless pork loin

1 large sweet onion, halved and sliced

2 large tomatoes, chopped

1 16-oz. jar salsa verde (green salsa)

½ cup dry white wine

4 cloves garlic, minced

1 tsp. cumin

½ tsp. chili powder

1. Place the pork loin in the crock and add the rest of the ingredients on top.

2. Cover and cook on low for 6 to 6½ hours.

3. Break apart the pork with two forks and mix with contents of crock.

Serving suggestion:

Serve over cooked brown rice or quinoa.

Protein: 25 g

Paprika Pork Chops with Rice

Sharon Easter, Yuba City, CA

Makes 4 servings

Prep. Time: 5 minutes   *Cooking Time: 30 minutes*

⅛ tsp. pepper

1 tsp. paprika

4–5 thick-cut boneless pork chops
(1 inch to 1½ inches thick)

1 Tbsp. olive oil

1¼ cups water, *divided*

1 onion, sliced 

½ green bell pepper, sliced in rings

1½ cups canned no-salt-added
stewed tomatoes

1 cup brown rice

1. Mix the pepper and paprika in a flat dish. Dredge the chops in the seasoning mixture.

2. Set the Instant Pot to Saute and heat the oil in the inner pot.

3. Brown the chops on both sides for 1 to 2 minutes a side. Remove the pork chops and set aside.

4. Pour a small amount of water into the inner pot and scrape up any bits from the bottom with a wooden spoon. Press Cancel.

5. Place the browned chops side by side in the inner pot. Place 1 slice of onion and 1 ring of green pepper on top of each chop. Spoon tomatoes with their juices over the top.

6. Pour the rice in and pour the remaining water over the top.

7. Secure the lid and set the vent to sealing.

8. Manually set the cook time for 30 minutes on high pressure.

9. When the cooking time is over, manually release the pressure.

Protein: 35 g

Raspberry Balsamic Pork Chops

Hope Comerford, Clinton Township, MI

Makes 4–6 servings
Prep. Time: 5 minutes   Cooking Time: 7–8 hours   Ideal slow-cooker size: 3-qt.

4–5 lb. thick-cut pork chops
¼ cup raspberry balsamic vinegar
2 Tbsp. olive oil
½ tsp. kosher salt
½ tsp. garlic powder
¼ tsp. basil
¼ cup water

1. Place pork chops in slow cooker.

2. In a small bowl, mix the remaining ingredients. Pour over the pork chops.

3. Cover and cook on low for 7 to 8 hours.

Serving suggestion:

Serve with Moroccan Sweet Potato Medley (page 187).

Protein: 64 g

Korean-Inspired BBQ Shredded Pork

Hope Comerford, Clinton Township, MI

Makes 8–10 servings
Prep. Time: 8–10 minutes & Cooking Time: 8–10 hours & Ideal slow-cooker size: 3-qt.

1 medium onion

1 McIntosh apple, peeled, cored

5 cloves garlic

¼ cup rice vinegar

1 tsp. gluten-free hot sauce

2 Tbsp. low-sodium gluten-free soy sauce

1 Tbsp. ginger

1 Tbsp. chili powder

¼ tsp. red pepper flakes

3 Tbsp. brown sugar

1 cup ketchup

2–3 lb. pork sirloin tip roast

1. In a food processor, puree the onion, apple, and garlic. Pour this mixture in a bowl and mix it with the rice vinegar, hot sauce, soy sauce, ginger, chili powder, red pepper flakes, brown sugar, and ketchup.

2. Place the pork roast into the crock. Pour the sauce over the top and turn it so it's covered on all sides.

3. Cover and cook on low for 8 to 10 hours.

4. Remove the pork roast and shred it between two forks. Return the shredded pork to the crock and mix it through the sauce.

Serving suggestion:

Serve over brown rice or quinoa with a side of bok choi sautéed in toasted sesame seed oil and red pepper flakes.

Protein: 30 g

Taylor's Favorite Szechuan Pork

Maria Shevlin, Sicklerville, NJ

Makes 3–4 servings
Prep. Time: 5 minutes   ❧   Cooking Time: 15 minutes

2 tsp. olive oil

4 thick boneless loin chops, sliced into thin strips

1 onion, sliced

1 cup water

1–2 heaping Tbsp. chili garlic paste

2 tsp. turbinado sugar

3 Tbsp. low-sodium tomato paste

1 tsp. coconut aminos or soy sauce

2–3 green onions, chopped, *optional*

Sesame seeds, *optional*

1. Set the Instant Pot to Saute and heat the olive oil.

2. Sauté the pork in the Instant Pot until lightly browned.

3. Toss in the onion; stir until mixed well.

4. Add the water, chili garlic paste, sugar, and tomato paste, and simmer until thickened.

5. Stir in the coconut aminos. Let simmer for 15 minutes.

6. Add as many green onions as you desire and mix well.

7. Top with the optional sesame seeds after plating.

Serving suggestion:

Serve with Quinoa and Black Beans (page 200).

Protein: 21 g

Philippine Ulam

Carol Eveleth, Cheyenne, WY

Makes 4–6 servings
Prep. Time: 25 minutes   Cooking Time: 30 minutes

2 lb. cubed pork chunks

¼ tsp. black pepper

1–2 Tbsp. oil

4 cups cubed potatoes

3 bell peppers, diced

¼ cup lemon juice

½ cup soy sauce

4 cups water

1. Sprinkle pork chunks with pepper.

2. Press Saute. When the word "hot" appears, swirl in oil in the inner pot.

3. Place the cubed pork chunks in the inner pot and cook 5 minutes, or until golden brown on all sides.

4. Add cubed potatoes, peppers, lemon juice, soy sauce, and water.

5. Close and lock the lid of the Instant Pot. Turn the steam release handle to sealing position. Cook on Manual at high pressure for 20 minutes. Allow a 10-minute natural pressure release. Turn steam release handle to Venting to release remaining pressure.

Serving suggestion:

Serve over cooked brown rice or quinoa.

Protein: 39 g

Delectable Eggplant

Thelma Good, Harrisonburg, VA

Makes 3 main-dish servings

Prep. Time: 20 minutes ❧ *Cooking Time: 10 minutes* ❧ *Cooling Time: 10 minutes*

2 tsp. olive oil

½ cup chopped onion

I small green bell pepper, chopped

I celery rib, chopped

I medium eggplant, peeled and chopped

¼ cup brown sugar

1½ tsp. dried basil

¼ tsp. garlic powder

¼ tsp. salt

2 (8-oz.) cans no-salt-added tomato sauce

I cup water

I cup low-fat shredded mozzarella cheese

3 slices bacon, cooked and crumbled, *divided*

¾ cup roasted pepitas, *divided*

1. Add 2 teaspoons of olive oil to a medium saucepan on the stove and heat over medium-high heat.

2. Sauté the onion, bell pepper, celery, and eggplant for about 8 minutes.

3. Stir in the brown sugar, basil, garlic powder, salt, and tomato sauce.

4. Pour the water into the inner pot of the Instant Pot and place the trivet on top.

5. Generously spray a 7-inch round baking pan with nonstick cooking spray.

6. Place half of the eggplant mixture into the round baking pan. Sprinkle with half the cheese.

7. Repeat layers. Garnish each bowl with a slice of crumbled bacon and ¼ cup roasted pepitas.

Protein: 20 g

Beef

Hungarian Beef with Paprika

Maureen Csikasz, Wakefield, MA

Makes 9 servings

Prep. Time: 15 minutes ⚶ *Cooking Time: 3–6 hours* ⚶ *Ideal slow-cooker size: oval 5- or 6-qt.*

3-lb. boneless chuck roast

2–3 medium onions, coarsely chopped

5 Tbsp. sweet paprika

¾ tsp. salt

¼ tsp. black pepper

½ tsp. caraway seeds

1 clove garlic, chopped

½ green bell pepper, sliced

¼ cup water

½ cup nonfat plain Greek yogurt

Fresh parsley

1. Grease interior of slow-cooker crock.

2. Place roast in crock.

3. In a good-sized bowl, mix all ingredients together, except nonfat plain Greek yogurt and parsley.

4. Spoon evenly over roast.

5. Cover. Cook on high for 3 to 4 hours, or on low for 5 to 6 hours, or until instant-read meat thermometer registers 140°F to 145°F when stuck in center of meat.

6. When finished cooking, use sturdy tongs or 2 metal spatulas to lift meat to cutting board. Cover with foil to keep warm. Let stand for 10 to 15 minutes.

7. Cut into chunks or slices.

8. Just before serving, dollop with nonfat plain Greek yogurt. Garnish with fresh parsley.

Serving suggestion:

Serve with Lentils and Barley (page 198).

Protein: 31 g

Espresso Braised Beef

Dena Mell-Dorchy, Royal Oak, MI

Makes 6 servings

Prep. Time: 25 minutes ❧ *Cooking Time: 8–9 hours* ❧ *Ideal slow-cooker size: 3- or 4-qt.*

1 large onion, cut into wedges

3 medium carrots, cut into ½-inch pieces

1 medium turnip, cut into 1-inch pieces

3 celery stalks, cut into 1-inch pieces

1½-lb. boneless beef chuck, cut into 1-inch pieces

⅔ cup gluten-free beef stock

2 Tbsp. tomato paste

1 Tbsp. instant espresso coffee powder

1 tsp. packed brown sugar

1 tsp. dried thyme

1 tsp. dried rosemary

½ tsp. sea salt

¼ tsp. pepper

1. Spray slow cooker with nonstick cooking spray.

2. In crock, combine onion, carrots, turnip, and celery. Top with beef.

3. Whisk together stock, tomato paste, espresso coffee powder, brown sugar, thyme, rosemary, salt, and pepper. Pour over beef and vegetables in crock.

4. Cover and cook on low for 8 to 9 hours.

Serving suggestion:

Serve over cooked brown rice or quinoa.

Protein: 23 g

Braised Beef with Cranberries

Audrey L. Kneer, Williamsfield, IL

Makes 8 servings
Prep. Time: 20 minutes   Cooking Time: 60 minutes

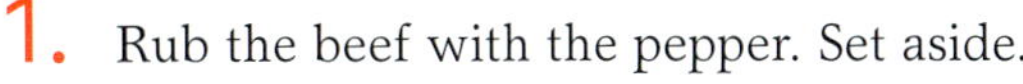

2-lb. sliced, well-trimmed top round beef

⅛ tsp. pepper

1 Tbsp. olive oil

1 medium onion, chopped

2 cloves garlic, chopped

½ cup peeled and diced turnip

1 medium carrot, chopped

1 celery rib, cut fine

1 cup low-sugar apple juice

1 cup fresh or frozen cranberries

1 sprig parsley

1 bay leaf

Serving suggestion:

Serve with Quinoa with Almonds and Cranberries (page 201).

1. Rub the beef with the pepper. Set aside.

2. Set the Instant Pot to Saute and heat the olive oil in the inner pot.

3. Sauté the beef for about 10 minutes, searing each side.

4. Remove the beef and set it aside.

5. Sauté the onion and garlic for about 3 minutes, then add the turnip, carrot, and celery and continue sautéing for about 5 more minutes.

6. Pour in the apple juice and scrape the bottom of the pot to deglaze.

7. Press Cancel. Add the beef back in, and add the cranberries, parsley, and bay leaf. Make sure the sprig of parsley and bay leaf are tucked into the liquid.

8. Secure the lid and set the vent to sealing.

9. Set the cook time manually for 60 minutes on high pressure.

10. When the cooking time is over, let the pressure release naturally for 10 minutes, then manually release the remaining pressure.

Protein: 34 g

Barbacoa Beef

Cindy Herren, West Des Moines, IA

Makes 6–8 servings
Prep. Time: 20 minutes   Cooking Time: 60 minutes

5 cloves garlic

½ medium onion

Juice of 1 lime

2–4 Tbsp. chipotles in adobo sauce (to taste)

1 tsp. ground cumin

1 tsp. ground oregano

½ tsp. ground cloves

1 cup water

3-lb. beef eye of round or bottom round roast

2½ tsp. kosher salt

Black pepper

1 tsp. oil

3 bay leaves

½ tsp. salt, *optional*

½ tsp. cumin, *optional*

Serving suggestion:

Serve over cooked brown rice or quinoa.

1. Place the garlic, onion, lime juice, chipotles, cumin, oregano, cloves, and water in a blender and puree until smooth.

2. Trim all the fat off the meat and then cut the meat into 3-inch pieces. Season with the salt and black pepper.

3. Set the Instant Pot to Saute. When hot, add the oil and brown the meat, in batches on all sides, about 5 minutes.

4. Press Cancel. Add all the browned meat, sauce from the blender, and bay leaves to the inner pot.

5. Secure the lid and set the vent to sealing.

6. Cook on high pressure for 60 minutes.

7. Manually release the pressure once cook time is up.

8. Remove the meat and place in a dish. Shred with two forks, and reserve 1½ cups of the liquid. Discard the bay leaves and the remaining liquid.

9. Return the shredded meat to the pot, add ½ teaspoon salt (or to taste), ½ tsp cumin, and 1½ cups of the reserved liquid.

Protein: 33 g

Stuffed Cabbage

Hope Comerford, Clinton Township, MI

Makes 12–15 stuffed cabbage rolls
Prep. Time: 30 minutes   Cooking Time: 20 minutes

13 cups water, *divided*

I large head cabbage (you will use about 12–15 leaves)

I lb. 95% lean ground beef

I medium onion, chopped

2 cloves garlic, chopped

I tsp. chopped fresh parsley

¼ tsp. salt

½ tsp. pepper

I egg, beaten

¾ cup uncooked brown rice

I Tbsp. vinegar

16 oz. low-sugar, low-sodium marinara sauce, *divided*

2 tsp. Italian seasoning

Variation:

You could make these with lean ground turkey instead of the beef, leave the meat out entirely, or replace with a meatless alternative such as crumbles.

Protein: 22 g

1. Pour 12 cups water into the inner pot and press Saute on the Instant Pot. Bring the water to a boil.

2. Gently lower the cabbage into the water and cook for about 5 minutes, turning to be sure all the outer leaves are softened. Press Cancel.

3. Remove the cabbage and carefully drain the water. Peel off 12 to 15 leaves.

4. In a bowl, mix the ground beef, onion, garlic, parsley, salt, pepper, egg, and brown rice with a wooden spoon or clean hands.

5. On a clean surface, lay out the cabbage leaves. (You may need to thin some of the thicker ribs of the cabbage leaves with a paring knife.) Evenly divide the filling between the leaves. Roll them burrito style, tucking in the ends and rolling tightly. If you need to, you can use a toothpick to hold them closed.

6. Pour 1 cup water and the vinegar into the inner pot. Gently place the cabbage rolls into the pot, pouring a little sauce on top of each layer and finishing with a layer of sauce. Sprinkle with the Italian seasoning.

7. Secure the lid and set the vent to sealing.

8. Set the Instant Pot to cook manually for 20 minutes on high pressure.

9. When the cooking time is over, let the pressure release naturally for 20 minutes and then manually release the remaining pressure.

10. When the pin drops, remove the lid. Serve hot.

Meatless

Mjadra (Lentils and Rice)

Hope Comerford, Clinton Township, MI

Makes 4–6 servings

Prep. Time: 1 hour, 20 minutes ⚬ *Cooking Time: 8 hours* ⚬ *Ideal slow-cooker size: 3-qt.*

½ cup olive oil

2 large sweet onions, chopped

1 cup dried lentils, rinsed

4 cups water

¼ cup lemon juice

⅛ tsp. pepper

1 tsp. salt

1 cup uncooked white rice

1. In a sauté pan on the stovetop, heat the olive oil over medium-high heat. Add the onions and let brown lightly. Reduce the heat to low and cover. Let the onions caramelize for at least 1 hour.

2. When the onions are done, add them and all the remaining ingredients to the crock and stir.

3. Cover and cook for 8 hours on low.

Serving suggestion:

Serve with whole wheat pita bread or on a bed of lettuce.

Protein: 11 g

Filled Acorn Squash

Teresa Martin, New Holland, PA

Makes 4 servings
Prep. Time: 20–30 minutes   ❧   Cooking Time: 5–11 hours   ❧   Ideal slow-cooker size: 7-qt.

2 medium acorn squash, about 1¼ lb. each

2 Tbsp. water

15-oz. can black beans, rinsed and drained

½ cup pine nuts, raw, or toasted if you have time

1 large tomato, coarsely chopped

2 green onions, thinly sliced

1 tsp. ground cumin

½ tsp. black pepper, *divided*

2 tsp. olive oil

½ cup reduced-fat shredded Monterey Jack cheese, *optional*

Serving suggestions:

Serve with Black Beans (page 190) and Hometown Spanish Rice (page 197).

1. Grease interior of slow-cooker crock.

2. Place washed whole squashes in slow cooker. Spoon in water.

3. Cover and cook on high for 4 to 6 hours or on low for 7 to 9 hours, or until squashes are tender when you pierce them with a fork.

4. While squashes are cooking, mix beans, pine nuts, tomato, green onions, cumin, and ¼ teaspoon black pepper. Set aside.

5. Use sturdy tongs or wear oven mitts to lift squashes out of cooker. Let cool until you can cut them in half and scoop out the seeds.

6. Brush cut sides and cavity of each squash half with olive oil.

7. Sprinkle all four cut sides with remaining black pepper.

8. Spoon heaping ½ cup of bean mixture into each halved squash, pressing down gently to fill cavity.

9. Return halves to slow cooker. Cover and cook on high for another hour, or on low for another 2 hours, until vegetables are as tender as you like them and thoroughly hot.

10. Uncover and sprinkle with optional cheese just before serving. When cheese has melted, put a filled half squash on each diner's plate.

Protein: 21 g

Spaghetti with No-Meat Sauce

Becky Fixel, Grosse Pointe Farms, MI

Makes 6–8 servings
Prep. Time: 5 minutes ⚶ *Cooking Time: 6 hours* ⚶ *Ideal slow-cooker size: 7-qt.*

2 Tbsp. olive oil

28-oz. can crushed tomatoes

28-oz. can tomato sauce

15-oz. can Italian stewed tomatoes

6-oz. can tomato paste

2–3 Tbsp. basil

2 Tbsp. oregano

2 Tbsp. honey

2 Tbsp. garlic paste (or 2 large cloves, peeled and minced)

2 lb. meatless crumbles

1. Pour olive oil in the crock. Use a paper towel to rub it all around the inside.

2. Add all ingredients to crock. Mix.

3. Cover and cook on low for 6 hours.

Serving suggestion:

Serve over your favorite protein pasta.

Protein: 32 g

Mexi Rotini

Jane Geigley, Lancaster, PA

Makes 6 servings
Prep. Time: 30 minutes   Cooking Time: 4½ hours   Ideal slow-cooker size: 4-qt.

I cup water

3 cups partially cooked whole wheat rotini

12-oz. pkg. frozen mixed vegetables

10-oz. can Ro*Tel diced tomatoes with green chilies

4-oz. can green chilies, undrained

I lb. meatless crumbles

½ cup low-fat shredded cheddar cheese

1. Combine all ingredients in slow cooker except shredded cheddar.

2. Cover and cook on low for 4 hours.

3. Top with the low-fat shredded cheddar, then let cook covered for an additional 20 minutes or so.

Serving suggestion:

Serve with Hometown Spanish Rice (page 197).

Protein: 26 g

Insta Pasta à la Maria

Maria Shevlin, Sicklerville, NJ

Makes 6–8 servings
Prep. Time: 10–15 minutes   Cooking Time: 6 minutes

32-oz. jar of vegan spaghetti sauce
or 1 qt. of homemade

2 cups fresh chopped spinach

1 cup chopped mushrooms

16 oz. meatless crumbles

1 tsp. salt

½ tsp. black pepper

½ tsp. dried basil

¼ tsp. red pepper flakes

1 tsp. parsley flakes

13¼-oz. box protein pasta

3 cups water

1. Place the sauce in the bottom of the inner pot of the Instant Pot.

2. Add the spinach, then the mushrooms.

3. Add the meatless crumbles on top of the veggies and sauce.

4. Add the seasonings and give it a stir to mix.

5. Add the box of pasta.

6. Add 3 cups of water.

7. Secure the lid and move vent to sealing. Set to Manual on high pressure for 6 minutes.

8. When cook time is up, release the pressure manually.

9. Remove the lid and stir to mix.

Protein: 23 g

Pasta Primavera

Hope Comerford, Clinton Township, MI

Makes 6 servings

Prep. Time: 10 minutes ⚬ *Cooking Time: 5 minutes (may vary due to pasta chosen)*

2 cups chopped broccolini tops

½ lb. baby bella mushrooms, sliced

2 small zucchini, sliced into ¼-inch-thick rounds

1 cup sliced cherry tomatoes

3 cloves garlic, sliced

½ tsp. salt

⅛ tsp. pepper

2 Tbsp. olive oil, *divided*

8 oz. protein pasta, shape of your choice

4 cups reduced-sodium vegetable stock

¼ cup shredded Parmesan cheese

2 Tbsp. chopped fresh basil

1. In a large bowl, toss the broccolini, mushrooms, zucchini, cherry tomatoes, garlic, salt, and pepper with 1 tablespoon olive oil.

2. Set the Instant Pot to Saute and heat the additional tablespoon of olive oil.

3. Pour the vegetables into the inner pot. Stir regularly for about 7 minutes, or until the vegetables are tender. Put them back in the large bowl you had them in and cover to keep them warm.

4. Press Cancel. Pour the pasta and vegetable stock into the inner pot and secure the lid. Set the vent to sealing.

5. Manually set the cook time for 5 minutes on high pressure, or half of whatever time the package instructions say to cook your pasta of choice for.

6. When the cooking time is over, manually release the pressure.

7. When the pin drops, remove the lid. Use a ladle to remove 1 cup of the cooking liquid. Pour this into the bowl with vegetables.

8. Wearing oven mitts, carefully remove the inner pot and drain the pasta into a colander.

9. Pour the drained pasta into the large bowl with the reserved cooking liquid and vegetables. Add the Parmesan cheese and fresh basil. Toss and enjoy!

Protein: 12 g

Quinoa with Spinach

Karen Ceneviva, New Haven, CT

Makes 4 servings
Prep. Time: 7 minutes   Cooking Time: 1 minute

1½ cups raw quinoa

3 Tbsp. extra-virgin olive oil, *divided*

12 oz. meatless sausage crumbles

2¼ cups water

3 Tbsp. freshly squeezed lemon juice

¼ tsp. sea salt

Pepper to taste, *optional*

2 cups fresh spinach leaves, well washed, dried, and chopped

3 large green onions, thinly sliced

3 Tbsp. fresh dill

Serving suggestions:

Serve with Black Beans (page 190) or Perfect Pinto Beans (page 192).

1. Rinse and drain the quinoa. Set aside.

2. Set the Instant Pot to Saute and pour in 1 tablespoon olive oil. Let it heat up.

3. Add the meatless crumbles and sauté for 3 to 5 minutes.

4. Pour in the water and scrape the bottom with a wooden spoon to remove any stuck-on bits. Press Cancel.

5. Add the quinoa. Secure the lid and set the vent to sealing.

6. Manually set the time for 1 minute on high pressure.

7. When the cooking time is over, let the pressure release naturally.

8. When the pin drops, remove the lid. Stir in the lemon juice, 2 tablespoons olive oil, sea salt, and pepper (if using).

9. Stir in the spinach, green onions, and dill.

10. Serve warm or at room temperature.

Protein: 10 g

Spinach Pie

Mary Ellen Musser, Reinholds, PA

Makes 4 main-dish servings
Prep. Time: 5 minutes & Cooking Time: 25 minutes & Standing Time: 10 minutes

2 cups low-sodium fat-free
cottage cheese

10-oz. pkg. frozen chopped
spinach, thawed and squeezed dry

1 cup reduced-fat mozzarella
cheese, shredded

Egg substitute equivalent to 4 eggs,
or 8 egg whites, beaten

⅓ cup (1½ oz.) grated low-fat
Parmesan cheese

1 tsp. dried oregano

1 cup water

1. Mix all the ingredients in a large bowl.

2. Spoon into a lightly greased 7-inch round pan. Cover it tightly with foil.

3. Pour the water into the inner pot of the Instant Pot. Place the trivet on top.

4. Place the filled pan on top of the trivet.

5. Secure the lid and set the vent to sealing.

6. Manually set the cook time to 25 minutes on high pressure.

7. When the cooking time is over, let the pressure release naturally for 10 minutes, then manually release the remaining pressure.

8. When the pin drops, remove the lid and carefully lift the trivet and pan out with oven mitts. Remove the foil. Allow to stand for 10 minutes before cutting.

Protein: 35 g

Bell Pepper Casserole

Janie Steele, Moore, OK

Makes 6 servings
Prep. Time: 10 minutes & Cooking Time: 10 minutes

16 oz. meatless crumbles

1 Tbsp. olive oil

3–4 bell peppers, diced
(your choice of colors)

½ cup diced onion

¾ cup long-grain rice

6-oz. can diced chilies

14-oz. can diced tomatoes

24-oz. jar vegan marinara sauce

½ tsp. chili powder

1 tsp. seasoned salt

2–3 cloves garlic, minced

1. Using the Saute function, sauté the meatless crumbles in the olive oil in inner pot of the Instant Pot.

2. Add the peppers and onion, then press Cancel.

3. Add the remaining ingredients. Do not stir.

4. Secure the lid and make sure vent is at sealing. Turn the Instant Pot on Manual for 10 minutes.

5. Let the pressure release naturally.

Serving suggestion:

Serve with Artichoke and Brown Rice (page 195).

Protein: 22 g

Uniquely Stuffed Peppers

Maria Shevlin, Sicklerville, NJ

Makes 4 servings
Prep. Time: 20–30 minutes & *Cooking Time: 15 minutes*

4 red bell peppers

1 tsp. olive oil

½ onion, chopped

3 cloves garlic, minced

8 oz. meatless crumbles

8 oz. spicy meatless sausage crumbles

1 tsp. salt

½ tsp. black pepper

1 tsp. garlic powder

½ tsp. dried oregano

½ tsp. dried basil

1 medium zucchini, grated and water pressed out

½ cup vegan barbecue sauce

¼ cup quick oats

1 cup water or vegetable broth

1. Cut the stem part of the top off the bell peppers, remove seeds and membranes, and set aside.

2. Add olive oil, onion, and garlic to a pan. Cook till al dente.

3. Add all meatless crumbles and brown lightly.

4. Add the seasonings, zucchini, and barbecue sauce.

5. Add the oats.

6. Mix well to combine.

7. Stuff the filling inside each pepper—pack it in.

8. Add 1 cup of water or vegetable broth to the bottom of the inner pot of the Instant Pot.

9. Add the rack to the pot.

10. Arrange the stuffed peppers standing upright.

11. Lock lid, make sure vent is at sealing, and use the Manual setting to set for 15 minutes.

12. When cook time is up, release the pressure manually.

Protein: 27 g

Mild Tempeh Curry with Coconut Milk

Brittney Horst, Lititz, PA

Makes 4–6 servings
Prep. Time: 30 minutes   Cooking Time: 7 minutes

1 large onion, diced

6 cloves garlic, crushed

64 oz. extra-firm tofu, drained, pressed, and diced

¼ cup coconut oil or avocado oil

½ tsp. black pepper

½ tsp. turmeric

½ tsp. paprika

¼ tsp. cinnamon

¼ tsp. cloves

¼ tsp. cumin

¼ tsp. ginger

½ tsp. salt

1 Tbsp. curry powder (more if you like more flavor)

½ tsp. chili powder

24-oz. can diced or crushed tomatoes

13½-oz. can coconut milk (I prefer a brand that has no unwanted ingredients, like guar gum or sugar)

1. Sauté onion, garlic, and tofu in oil in the inner pot of the Instant Pot on Saute setting.

2. Combine spices in a small bowl, then add to the inner pot.

3. Add tomatoes and coconut milk and stir.

4. Secure the lid and make sure vent is at sealing. Set to Manual mode (or Pressure Cook on newer models) for 2 minutes.

5. Let pressure release naturally (if you're crunched for time, you can do a quick release).

6. Serve with your favorite sides, and enjoy!

Serving suggestion:

Serve with cooked brown rice, or quinoa, and a side of veggies.

Protein: 30 g

Teriyaki Tempeh Steaks with Sugar Snap Peas

Hope Comerford, Clinton Township, MI

Makes 4–6 servings

Prep. Time: 10 minutes   Cooking Time: 5 hours   Ideal slow-cooker size: 5-qt.

3 (8-oz.) blocks of tempeh

I Tbsp. onion powder, *divided*

I Tbsp. garlic powder, *divided*

Salt to taste

Pepper to taste

I cup coconut aminos

15 drops liquid stevia

½ Tbsp. flaxseed

½ medium onion, sliced into half rings

1½–2 cups sugar snap peas

Serving suggestion:

Serve with cooked brown rice or quinoa.

1. Place the tempeh blocks in the crock and sprinkle them with half the onion powder, half the garlic powder, and a bit of salt and pepper.

2. Mix together the coconut aminos, liquid stevia, and flaxseed.

3. Pour half of the coconut aminos sauce over the contents of the crock.

4. Place the onion slices on top and sprinkle them with more salt, pepper, and the rest of the garlic powder and onion powder. Pour the rest of the coconut aminos sauce over the top.

5. Cover and cook on low for 5 hours.

6. About 40 minutes before the cook time is up, add the sugar snap peas.

7. Serve the tempeh with some of the sugar snap peas on top and sauce from the crock drizzled over the top.

Protein: 31 g

Savory Slow-Cooker Tempeh

Sara Harter Fredette, Williamsburg, MA

Makes 4 servings

Prep. Time: 25 minutes ❧ *Cooking Time: 5 hours* ❧ *Ideal slow-cooker size: 4- or 5-qt.*

2 (8-oz.) pkg. tempeh, each sliced into 2 pieces

1 lb. fresh tomatoes, chopped, or 15-oz. can stewed tomatoes

1 bay leaf

¼ tsp. pepper

2 cloves garlic, minced

1 onion, chopped

½ cup vegan vegetable broth

1 tsp. dried thyme

¼ tsp. salt

2 cups broccoli, cut into bite-size pieces

1. Combine all ingredients except broccoli in slow cooker.

2. Cover. Cook on low for 5 hours.

3. Add broccoli 30 minutes before serving.

Serving suggestion:

Serve with Mushroom Risotto (page 193).

Protein: 26 g

Seafood

Spiced Cod

Hope Comerford, Clinton Township, MI

Makes 4–6 servings

Prep. Time: 8 minutes ❧ *Cooking Time: 2 hours* ❧ *Ideal slow-cooker size: 4- or 5-qt.*

4–6 cod fillets

½ cup thinly sliced red onion

1½ tsp. garlic powder

1½ tsp. onion powder

½ tsp. cumin

¼ tsp. ancho chili powder

1 lime, juiced

⅓ cup vegetable broth

1. Place fish in the crock. Place the onion on top.

2. Mix together the remaining ingredients and pour over the fish.

3. Cover and cook on low for 2 hours, or until fish flakes easily with a fork.

Serving suggestion:

Serve over cooked quinoa or brown rice.

Protein: 42 g

Herbed Flounder

Dorothy VanDeest, Memphis, TX

Makes 6 servings
Prep. Time: 10 minutes   Cooking Time: 2–3 hours   Ideal slow-cooker size: 6-qt.

2 lb. flounder fillets, fresh or frozen

¾ cup gluten-free, low-sodium chicken broth or stock

2 Tbsp. lemon juice

2 Tbsp. dried chives

2 Tbsp. dried minced onion

½–1 tsp. leaf marjoram

4 Tbsp. chopped fresh parsley

½ tsp. sea salt

1. Wipe fish as dry as possible. Cut fish into portions to fit slow cooker.

2. Combine broth and lemon juice. Stir in remaining ingredients.

3. Cover and cook on high for 2 to 3 hours, or until fish is flaky.

Serving suggestion:

Serve over cooked brown rice or quinoa.

Protein: 26 g

Lemon Pepper Tilapia

Karen Ceneviva, New Haven, CT

Makes 4 servings
Prep. Time: 1 minute ✄ *Cooking Time: 2–4 minutes*

1 cup water

4 (6-oz.) tilapia fillets, fresh or frozen

2 tsp. lemon pepper seasoning

1. Pour the water into the inner pot of the Instant Pot.

2. Sprinkle the fillets with lemon pepper seasoning on both sides.

3. Place the steamer basket into the inner pot and carefully arrange the tilapia in the basket.

4. Secure the lid and set the vent to sealing.

5. Manually set the cook time for 2 minutes on high pressure for fresh fish, or 4 minutes for frozen fish.

6. When the cooking time is over, manually release the pressure.

7. When the pin drops, remove the lid. Make sure the fish is at 145°F.

Serving suggestion:

Serve with Lentils and Barley (page 198).

Protein: 34 g

Lemon Dijon Fish

June S. Groff, Denver, PA

Makes 4 servings

Prep. Time: 10 minutes   *Cooking Time: 3 hours*   *Ideal slow-cooker size: 2-qt.*

1½ lb. orange roughy fillets
2 Tbsp. Dijon mustard
3 Tbsp. olive oil, melted
1 tsp. Worcestershire sauce
1 Tbsp. lemon juice

1. Cut fillets to fit in slow cooker.

2. In a bowl, mix remaining ingredients. Pour over fish. (If you have to stack the fish, spoon a portion of the sauce over the first layer of fish before adding the second layer.)

3. Cover and cook on low for 3 hours, or until fish flakes easily but is not dry or overcooked.

Serving suggestion:

Serve with Quinoa and Black Beans (page 200).

Protein: 32 g

Greek-Style Halibut Steaks

Kristi See, Weskan, KS

Makes 4 servings
Prep. Time: 10 minutes   Cooking Time: 3 minutes

1 tsp. olive oil

1 cup unpeeled diced zucchini

½ cup minced onion

1 clove garlic, peeled and minced

2 cups diced fresh tomatoes

2 Tbsp. chopped fresh basil

¼ tsp. salt

¼ tsp. pepper

4 (6-oz.) halibut steaks

⅓ cup crumbled reduced-fat feta cheese

1 cup water

1. Set the Instant Pot to Saute and heat the olive oil in the inner pot.

2. Sauté the zucchini, onion, and garlic for 5 minutes.

3. Mix in the tomatoes, basil, salt, and pepper. Press Cancel.

4. In a 7-inch round baking pan, arrange the halibut steaks. Using oven mitts, carefully pour the zucchini mixture from the inner pot over the halibut. Top with the feta cheese.

5. Quickly wipe out the inner pot. Pour in the water and place the trivet on top.

6. Place the baking pan on top of the trivet in the inner pot. Secure the lid and set the vent to sealing.

7. Manually set the cook time for 3 minutes on high pressure.

8. When the cooking time is over, manually release the pressure.

9. When the pin drops, remove the lid and carefully take the trivet out with oven mitts. Make sure the fish has reached 145°F. Serve halibut and enjoy!

Serving suggestion:

Serve with White Beans with Sun-Dried Tomatoes (page 189).

Protein: 36 g

Salmon with Chives

Gloria Julien, Gladstone, MI

Makes 2 servings
Prep. Time: 5 minutes ⚶ *Cooking Time: 3–5 minutes*

I cup water

2 (5-oz.) pieces salmon with skin

2 tsp. extra-virgin olive oil

I Tbsp. chopped chives

I Tbsp. fresh tarragon leaves, *optional*

1. Pour the water into the inner pot of the Instant Pot and place the trivet on top.

2. Line a 7-inch round baking pan with foil.

3. Rub the salmon all over with the oil.

4. Place the salmon skin-side down on the foil. Place the baking pan on top of the trivet in the inner pot.

5. Secure the lid and set the vent to sealing.

6. Manually set the cook time on high pressure for 3 minutes if fresh or 5 minutes if frozen.

7. When the cooking time is over, manually release the pressure.

8. When the pin drops, remove the lid and carefully remove the trivet from the inner pot with oven mitts. Check to make sure the fillet is at 145°F.

9. Using a metal spatula, lift salmon off skin and place salmon on serving plate. Discard skin.

10. Sprinkle salmon with herbs and serve.

Serving suggestion:

Serve with Herbed Rice Pilaf (page 196).

Protein: 30 g

Wild Salmon with Capers

Bernita Boyts, Shawnee Mission, KS

Makes 4 servings

Prep. Time: 15 minutes ❖ Cooking Time: 3–5 minutes

I cup water

I tsp. olive oil

I lb. wild salmon fillet

Salt to taste

Black pepper to taste

2 Tbsp. butter or margarine

I clove garlic, chopped fine

¼ cup white wine or water

2 Tbsp. capers

2 green onions, finely chopped

I tsp. fresh dill weed

I medium tomato, chopped

I Tbsp. lemon juice

Serving suggestion:

Serve with Artichokes and Brown Rice (page 195).

Protein: 24 g

1. Pour the water into the inner pot of the Instant Pot. Place the trivet on top.

2. In a 7-inch round baking pan, spread the olive oil on the bottom.

3. Season the salmon fillet with salt and pepper and lay it skin-side down in the baking pan.

4. Place the baking pan on top of the trivet in the inner pot.

5. Secure the lid and set the vent to sealing.

6. Manually set the cook time on high pressure for 3 minutes if fresh or 5 minutes if frozen.

7. When the cooking time is over, manually release the pressure. Press Cancel.

8. When the pin drops, remove the lid and carefully remove the trivet from the inner pot with oven mitts. Check to make sure the fillet is at 145°F. Cover the fish to keep it warm.

9. Carefully pour the water out of the inner pot and quickly wipe dry.

10. Set the Instant Pot to Sauté and melt the butter in the inner pot. Add the garlic. Stir and cook for about 30 seconds.

11. Add the wine and heat until bubbling, scraping brown bits into liquid.

12. Add the capers, green onions, and dill. Cook for another minute.

13. Stir in the chopped tomato. Heat through.

14. Sprinkle the lemon juice over the salmon. Top with the sauce and serve.

Honey Lemon Garlic Salmon

Judy Gascho, Woodburn, OR

Makes 4 servings
Prep. Time: 15 minutes   *Cooking Time: 5–12 minutes*

5 Tbsp. olive oil

3 Tbsp. honey

2–3 Tbsp. lemon juice

3 cloves garlic, minced

4 (3- or 4-oz.) fresh salmon fillets

Salt to taste

Pepper to taste

1–2 Tbsp. minced parsley
(dried or fresh)

Lemon slices, *optional*

1½ cups water

Serving suggestion:
Serve with Quinoa and Black
Beans (page 200).

1. Mix olive oil, honey, lemon juice, and minced garlic in a bowl.

2. Place each salmon fillet on a piece of foil big enough to wrap up the piece of fish.

3. Brush each fillet generously with the olive oil mixture.

4. Sprinkle with salt, pepper, and parsley flakes.

5. Top each with a thin slice of lemon if desired.

6. Wrap each fillet and seal well at top.

7. Place 1½ cups of water in the inner pot of the Instant Pot and place the trivet in the pot.

8. Place wrapped fillets on the trivet.

9. Close the lid and turn valve to sealing.

10. Cook on Manual at high pressure for 5 to 8 minutes for smaller pieces, or for 10 to 12 minutes if they are large.

11. Carefully release pressure at the end of the cooking time manually.

12. Unwrap and enjoy.

Protein: 26 g

Maple-Glazed Salmon

Jenelle Miller, Marion, SD

Makes 6 servings
Prep. Time: 5 minutes   *Cooking Time: 3 minutes*

2 tsp. paprika

2 tsp. chili powder

½ tsp. ground cumin

½ tsp. brown sugar

½ tsp. kosher salt

6 (4-oz) salmon fillets

1 Tbsp. maple syrup

1 cup water

Serving suggestion:

Serve with Quinoa with Almonds and Cranberries (page 201).

1. In a small bowl, combine the first five ingredients.

2. Rub the fillets with the seasoning mixture.

3. Spray a 7-inch round baking pan with nonstick cooking spray, and place the salmon in the pan skin-side down. Drizzle the fish with the maple syrup.

4. Pour the water into the inner pot of the Instant Pot and place the trivet on top.

5. Secure the lid and set the vent to sealing.

6. Manually set the cook time for 3 minutes on high pressure.

7. When the cooking time is over, manually release the pressure.

8. When the pin drops, remove the lid and carefully remove the trivet from the inner pot with oven mitts. Check to make sure the fillets are at 145°F.

Protein: 23 g

Side Dishes

Moroccan Sweet Potato Medley

Pat Bishop, Bedminster, PA

Makes 6 servings
Prep. Time: 20 minutes & Cooking Time: 2¼–3¼ hours & Ideal slow-cooker size: 4-qt.

1 medium onion, sliced

2 tsp. olive oil

2 cloves garlic, minced

1½ tsp. ground coriander

1½ tsp. cumin

¼ tsp. cayenne pepper

2 medium sweet potatoes, peeled, cut into ½-inch slices, and cooked, or canned sweet potatoes, drained

14-oz. can stewed tomatoes

¾ cup uncooked bulgur

2¼ cups water

15-oz. can chickpeas, rinsed and drained

½ cup raisins

1 cup fresh cilantro leaves

1. Sauté onion in oil in small skillet until onion is tender.

2. Combine with garlic, coriander, cumin, cayenne pepper, sweet potatoes, tomatoes, bulgur, and water in 4-quart slow cooker.

3. Cover. Cook on low for 2 to 3 hours, or until water is absorbed.

4. Stir in chickpeas, raisins, and cilantro. Cook 15 more minutes.

5. Serve.

Tip:

Adjust the amount of cayenne pepper to suit your taste.

Serving suggestions:

Serve alongside Turkey with Mushroom Sauce (page 124), Turkey Meat Loaf (page 178), and Raspberry Balsamic Pork Chops (page 136).

Protein: 11 g

Beans 'n' Greens

Teri Sparks, Glen Burnie, MD

Makes 10 servings
Prep. Time: 30 minutes   &   Cooking Time: 6–8 hours   &   Ideal slow-cooker size: 4- or 5-qt.

1 lb. dried 13-bean mix
5 cups gluten-free vegetable broth
¼ cup green onions, chopped
½ tsp. black pepper
2 Tbsp. dried parsley
1 yellow onion, coarsely chopped
3 cloves garlic, chopped
1 Tbsp. olive oil
6 cups fresh kale, torn in 2-inch pieces
Greek yogurt

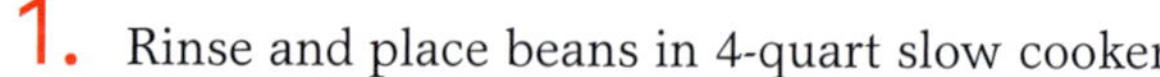

1. Rinse and place beans in 4-quart slow cooker.

2. Add broth, green onions, pepper, and parsley.

3. In skillet, sauté yellow onion and garlic in oil. Add to beans in slow cooker.

4. Pile kale on top of bean mixture and cover with lid (crock will be very full).

5. Cook on high for 1 hour. Greens will have wilted some, so stir to combine all ingredients. Replace lid. Cook on low for 6 to 8 hours.

6. Top individual servings with dollops of Greek yogurt.

Serving suggestion:

Serve alongside Rotisserie Chicken (page 99).

Protein: 6 g

White Beans with Sun-Dried Tomatoes

Steven Lantz, Denver, CO

Makes 4–6 servings
Soaking Time: 8 hours   Prep. Time: 15 minutes
Cooking Time: 4–6 hours   Ideal slow-cooker size: 4-qt.

2 cups uncooked great northern beans, soaked overnight, rinsed

2 cloves garlic, minced or pressed

1 onion, chopped

6 cups water

½ tsp. salt

⅛ tsp. pepper

1 cup chopped sun-dried tomatoes in oil, drained

2-oz. can sliced black olives, drained

¼ cup low-fat grated Parmesan cheese

1. Mix all ingredients except tomatoes, olives, and cheese in 4- or 5-quart slow cooker.

2. Cover and cook on high for 4 to 6 hours or until beans are tender.

3. Mash some of the beans to thicken mixture. Stir in tomatoes and olives. Cook for 20 to 30 minutes more, until thoroughly heated.

4. Ladle into bowls and sprinkle each with Parmesan cheese.

Serving suggestions:

Serve alongside Italian Chicken and Broccoli (page 102) and Greek-Style Halibut Steaks (page 178).

Protein: 8 g

Black Beans

Hope Comerford, Clinton Township, MI

Makes 10 servings
Prep. Time: 10 minutes 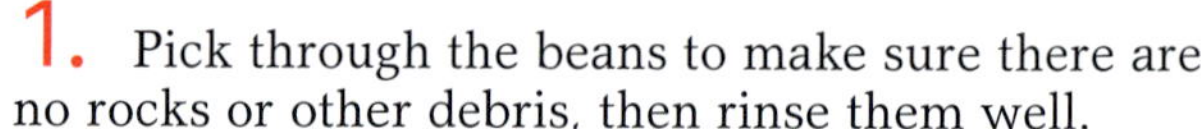 *Cooking Time: 25 minutes*

I lb. dry black beans

I cup chopped onion

3 cloves garlic

2 tsp. sea salt

¼ tsp. pepper

4 cups vegetable broth

2 cups water

1. Pick through the beans to make sure there are no rocks or other debris, then rinse them well.

2. Place the beans, onion, garlic, sea salt, and pepper into the inner pot of the Instant Pot.

3. Pour the broth and water over the top.

4. Secure the lid and set the vent to sealing. Manually set the cook time for 25 minutes on high pressure.

5. When cook time is up, let the pressure release naturally.

Serving suggestions:

Serve alongside Filled Acorn Squash (page 154) and Quinoa with Spinach (page 161).

Protein: 10 g

Perfect Pinto Beans

Hope Comerford, Clinton Township, MI

Makes 8 servings
Prep. Time: 2 minutes & Cooking Time: 50 minutes

I large onion, chopped

I lb. dry pinto beans, sorted and rinsed

6 cups low-sodium vegetable or chicken broth

2 bay leaves

1½ tsp. sea salt

I tsp. cumin

½ tsp. paprika

¼ tsp. pepper

1. Place all ingredients into the inner pot of the Instant Pot.

2. Secure the lid and set the vent to sealing. Manually set the cook time for 50 minutes on high pressure.

3. When the cook time is over, let the pressure release naturally for 15 minutes, then manually release the remaining pressure.

4. Remove and discard bay leaves before serving.

Serving suggestions:

Serve alongside Garlic Mushroom Thighs (page 104), Chicken Dijon Dinner (page 105), and Quinoa with Spinach (page 161).

Protein: 12 g

Mushroom Risotto

Hope Comerford, Clinton Township, MI

Makes 4 servings

Prep. Time: 7 minutes   Cooking Time: 6 minutes

1 Tbsp. extra-virgin olive oil

½ cup finely chopped onion

2 cloves garlic, minced

½ cup chopped baby bella mushrooms

½ cup chopped shiitake mushrooms

¼ tsp. salt

⅛ tsp. pepper

1 cup uncooked arborio rice

2 cups low-sodium chicken stock

½ cup frozen peas, thawed

¼ cup freshly grated low-fat Parmesan cheese

1 Tbsp. butter or margarine, *optional*

1. Set the Instant Pot to Saute and heat the oil in the inner pot.

2. Sauté the onion and garlic for 3 minutes. Add the mushrooms, salt, and pepper, and continue sautéing for an additional 3 to 4 minutes.

3. Press Cancel. Stir in the rice and chicken stock. Secure the lid and set the vent to sealing.

4. Manually set the cook time for 6 minutes on high pressure.

5. When the cooking time is over, manually release the pressure.

6. When the pin drops, remove the lid and stir in the peas, grated Parmesan, and butter (if using). Let the peas heat through for about 2 minutes, then serve.

Serving suggestions:

Serve alongside Italian Crockpot Chicken (page 101), Savory Slow-Cooker Tempeh (page 169), and Thyme and Garlic Turkey Breast (page 123).

Protein: 8 g

Artichokes and Brown Rice

Betty K. Drescher, Quakertown, PA

Makes 6 servings
Prep. Time: 5 minutes   Cooking Time: 15 minutes

1 Tbsp. extra-virgin olive oil

14.5-oz. can artichokes, drained
and cut into chunks

1 cup raw brown rice

1 cup low-sodium vegetable stock

1. Set the Instant Pot to Saute and heat the oil in the inner pot.

2. Sauté the artichokes in the olive oil for about 5 minutes. Press Cancel.

3. Add the rice and vegetable stock to the inner pot. Secure the lid and set the vent to sealing.

4. Manually set the cook time for 15 minutes on high pressure.

5. When the cooking time is over, let the pressure release naturally for 5 minutes, then manually release the remaining pressure.

6. When the pin drops, remove the lid and fluff the rice with a fork. Serve and enjoy!

Serving suggestions:

Serve alongside Rotisserie Chicken (page 99), Bell Pepper Casserole (page 163), and Wild Salmon with Capers (page 181).

Protein: 5 g

Herbed Rice Pilaf

Betty K. Drescher, Quakertown, PA

Makes 6 servings
Prep. Time: 10 minutes   Cooking Time: 22 minutes

I Tbsp. olive oil

½ cup chopped onion

I cup chopped celery

I ½ cups raw brown rice

I ¾ cups low-sodium, fat-free chicken broth

¾ tsp. Worcestershire sauce

¾ tsp. reduced-sodium soy sauce

¾ tsp. dried oregano

¾ tsp. dried thyme

1. Set the Instant Pot to Saute and heat the oil in the inner pot.

2. Add the onion and celery to the inner pot and sauté for about 5 minutes. Add the rice and lightly toast, about 1 minute. Press Cancel.

3. Add the broth, Worcestershire sauce, soy sauce, oregano, and thyme. Secure the lid and set the vent to sealing.

4. Manually set the time for 22 minutes on high pressure.

5. When the cooking time is over, let the pressure release naturally.

6. When the pin drops, remove the lid and fluff the rice with a fork. Serve and enjoy!

Serving suggestions:

Serve alongside Honey Balsamic Chicken (page 108), Thyme and Garlic Turkey Breast (page 123), and Salmon with Chives (page 179).

Protein: 6 g

Hometown Spanish Rice

Beverly Flatt-Getz, Warriors Mark, PA

Makes 6–8 servings
Prep. Time: 8 minutes ⚬ Cooking Time: 3 minutes

1 Tbsp. olive oil

1 large onion, chopped

1 bell pepper, chopped

2 cups long-grain rice, rinsed

1 ½ cups low-sodium chicken stock

28-oz. can low-sodium stewed tomatoes

Grated Parmesan cheese, *optional*

Serving suggestions:

Serve alongside Mexi Rotini (page 156) and Filled Acorn Squash (page 154).

1. Set the Instant Pot to Saute and heat the oil in the inner pot.

2. Sauté the onion and bell pepper in the inner pot for about 3 to 5 minutes.

3. Add the rice and continue to sauté for about 1 more minute. Press Cancel.

4. Add the chicken stock and tomatoes with their juices into the inner pot, in that order.

5. Secure the lid and set the vent to sealing.

6. Manually set the cook time for 3 minutes on high pressure.

7. When the cooking time is over, let the pressure release naturally for 10 minutes, then manually release the remaining pressure.

8. When the pin drops, remove the lid. Fluff the rice with a fork.

9. Sprinkle with Parmesan cheese, if using, just before serving.

Protein: 7 g

Lentils and Barley

Linda Yoder, Fresno, OH

Makes 3–4 servings
Prep. Time: 5 minutes & Cooking Time: 3–4 hours & Ideal slow-cooker size: 3-qt.

3 cups vegetable broth

1 cup uncooked lentils, rinsed and drained

3 Tbsp. olive oil

½ cup uncooked barley, rolled or pearl

1 large onion, chopped

1 clove garlic, minced

¼ lb. fresh mushrooms, cleaned and sliced, *optional*

1 Tbsp. Worcestershire sauce

1 tsp. dried thyme

⅛ tsp. ground pepper

Salt to taste

2 Tbsp. chopped fresh parsley

Extra-virgin olive oil for garnish

1. Place all ingredients into the crock and stir.

2. Cover and cook on low for 3 to 4 hours.

Tips:

1. If using pearl barley, you may need to increase the cooking time by 30 to 60 more minutes.

2. The olive oil garnish is the "frosting on the cake" for this recipe.

Serving suggestions:

Serve alongside Hungarian Beef with Paprika (page 145) and Lemon Pepper Tilapia (page 175).

Protein: 16 g

Quinoa and Black Beans

Gloria Frey, Lebanon, PA

Makes 6–8 servings
Prep. Time: 15 minutes ❧ *Cooking Time: 2–3 hours* ❧ *Ideal slow-cooker size: 4-qt.*

1 onion, chopped

3 cloves garlic, chopped

1 red bell pepper, chopped

1 tsp. olive oil

¾ cup uncooked quinoa

1½ cups vegetable broth

1 tsp. ground cumin

¼ tsp. cayenne pepper

Salt to taste

Pepper to taste

1 cup frozen corn

2 (15-oz.) cans black beans,
rinsed and drained

½ cup fresh cilantro, chopped

1. Sauté onion, garlic, and red bell pepper in olive oil in skillet until softened. Place in 4-quart slow cooker.

2. Mix quinoa into the vegetables and cover with vegetable broth.

3. Season with cumin, cayenne pepper, salt, and pepper.

4. Cover. Cook on low for 1 to 2 hours until quinoa is done.

5. Stir frozen corn, beans, and cilantro into cooker and continue to cook on low for 30 to 60 minutes until heated through.

Serving suggestions:

Serve alongside Taylor's Favorite Szechuan Pork (page 139), Lemon Dijon Fish (page 176), and Honey Lemon Garlic Salmon (page 182).

Protein: 13 g

Quinoa with Almonds and Cranberries

Colleen Heatwole, Burton, MI

Makes 4 servings
Prep. Time: 5 minutes   Cooking Time: 2 minutes

I cup quinoa, rinsed well

½ cup roasted slivered almonds

I vegetable bouillon cube

1½ cups water

¼ tsp. salt, *optional*

I cinnamon stick

½ cup dried cranberries or cherries

I bay leaf

1. Add all ingredients to the inner pot of the Instant Pot.

2. Secure the lid and make sure vent is on sealing. Cook 2 minutes using high pressure in Manual Mode.

3. Turn off pot and let the pressure release naturally for 10 minutes. After 10 minutes are up, release pressure manually.

4. Remove cinnamon stick and bay leaf.

5. Fluff with fork and serve.

Serving suggestions:

Serve alongside Maple-Glazed Salmon (page 183), Asian-Style Chicken with Pineapple (page 110), Savory Pork Roast (page 133), and Braised Beef with Cranberries (page 147).

Protein: 9 g

Cauliflower Cassoulet

Susie Shenk Wenger, Lancaster, PA

Makes 6 servings

Prep. Time: 30 minutes ❧ Cooking Time: 4–6 hours ❧ Ideal slow-cooker size: 6-qt.

1 cup uncooked brown rice

½ tsp. kosher salt

2 cups water

1 cup sliced fresh mushrooms

1 large sweet onion, chopped

½ cup chopped red bell pepper

3 cloves garlic, chopped

1 Tbsp. vegan butter

1 Tbsp. olive oil

1 large head cauliflower, chopped

½ cup nutritional yeast

1 tsp. dried basil

½ tsp. dried oregano

Salt to taste

Pepper to taste

Juice and zest of 1 lemon

1. Put rice and ½ teaspoon salt in lightly greased slow cooker. Pour water over rice.

2. Sprinkle in mushrooms, onion, bell pepper, and garlic. Sprinkle lightly with salt and pepper. Dot with vegan butter and drizzle with olive oil.

3. Sprinkle in cauliflower and nutritional yeast. Sprinkle with basil and oregano, adding salt and pepper to taste.

4. Cover and cook on low for 4 to 6 hours, until rice is cooked and cauliflower is tender.

5. Drizzle with lemon juice and zest before serving.

Serving suggestions:

Serve alongside Rotisserie Chicken (page 99) and Thyme and Garlic Turkey Breast (page 123).

Protein: 6 g

Desserts

Chocolate Mousse

Meg Suter, Goshen, IN

Makes 8 servings

Prep. Time: 10 minutes   *Cooking Time: 1–2 minutes*   *Chilling Time: 2–4 hours*

2 (12-oz.) bags dairy-free semisweet chocolate chips

15-oz. container silken tofu

1. Place chocolate chips in microwaveable bowl. Microwave in 30-second increments, stirring and checking each time until chocolate is melted.

2. Combine melted chocolate and tofu in a blender. Blend until smooth.

3. Refrigerate in serving bowl or individual glass dishes until well chilled. Serve.

Protein: 7 g

Lotsa Chocolate Almond Cake

Hope Comerford, Clinton Township, MI

Makes 10 servings
Prep. Time: 10 minutes   Cooking Time: 3 hours   Cooling Time: 30 minutes

4 Tbsp. ground flaxseed

¾ cup water

1½ cups almond flour

¾ cup turbinado sugar

⅔ cup cocoa powder

¼ cup vegan chocolate protein powder

2 tsp. baking powder

¼ tsp. salt

½ cup coconut oil, melted

¾ cup almond milk

1 tsp. vanilla extract

1 tsp. almond extract

¾ cup vegan dark chocolate chips

1. Mix together the flaxseed and water in a bowl and set aside to thicken, approximately 3 minutes.

2. Cover any hot spot of the crock with aluminum foil, and spray crock with vegan nonstick spray.

3. In a bowl, mix the almond flour, sugar, cocoa powder, protein powder, baking powder, and salt.

4. In a different bowl, mix the coconut oil, thickened flaxseed/water mixture, almond milk, and vanilla and almond extracts.

5. Pour wet ingredients into dry ingredients and mix until well combined. Stir in chocolate chips.

6. Pour cake mix into crock. Cover and cook on low for 3 hours.

7. Turn the slow cooker off when the cooking time is over and let the cake cool in the crock for 30 minutes.

8. Place a plate or platter over the crock, then turn the crock upside down on the plate, so the cake releases onto the plate or platter.

Protein: 10 g

Black Bean Brownies

Juanita Weaver, Johnsonville, IL

Makes 6–8 servings

Prep. Time: 5 minutes ❧ *Cooking Time: 1½ hours* ❧ *Ideal slow-cooker size: 5- or 6-qt.*

15-oz. can black beans, rinsed and drained

6 eggs

⅓ cup cocoa powder

1½ tsp. aluminum-free baking powder

½ tsp. baking soda

2 Tbsp. coconut oil

2 tsp. pure vanilla extract

⅓ cup nonfat Greek yogurt or nonfat cottage cheese

¾ cup xylitol or your choice of sweetener

¼ tsp. salt

1. Put all ingredients in a food processor or blender. Blend until smooth.

2. Pour into greased slow cooker.

3. Cover and cook for 1½ hours on high.

4. Cool in crock. For best taste, chill before serving.

Protein: 11 g

Zucchini Chocolate Chip Bars

Hope Comerford, Clinton Township, MI

Makes 8–10 servings
Prep Time: 10 minutes ⚜ *Cooking Time: 2–3 hours*
Cooling Time: 30 minutes ⚜ *Ideal slow-cooker size: 3-qt.*

3 eggs

¾ cup turbinado sugar

I cup all-natural applesauce

3 tsp. vanilla extract

I½ cups whole wheat flour

I½ cups vanilla whey protein concentrate

I tsp. baking soda

½ tsp. baking powder

2 tsp. cinnamon

¼ tsp. salt

2 cups peeled and grated zucchini

I cup dark chocolate chips

1. Spray the crock with nonstick cooking spray.

2. Mix together the eggs, sugar, applesauce, and vanilla.

3. In a separate bowl, mix the flour, whey protein, baking soda, baking powder, cinnamon, and salt. Add this to the wet mixture and stir just until everything is mixed well.

4. Stir in the zucchini and chocolate chips

5. Pour this mixture into the crock.

6. Cover and cook on low for 2 to 3 hours. Let it cool in crock for about 30 minutes, then flip it over onto a serving platter or plate. It should come right out.

Protein: 8 g

Rice Pudding

Betty Moore, Plano, IL

Makes 6 servings
Prep. Time: 8 minutes  Cooking Time: 25 minutes

I cup brown rice

½ cup raisins

I egg

3 egg whites

16 oz. fat-free evaporated milk

I cup water

⅓ cup brown sugar

I tsp. vanilla extract

⅛ tsp. nutmeg, *optional*

1. Pour the rice into the inner pot of the Instant Pot. Sprinkle the raisins over the top.

2. In a medium bowl, combine the egg, egg whites, milk, water, sugar, vanilla, and nutmeg (if using). Mix well. Pour this over the rice and raisins.

3. Secure the lid and set the vent to sealing.

4. Manually set the cook time for 25 minutes on high pressure.

5. When the cooking time is over, let the pressure release naturally.

6. When the pin drops, remove the lid and stir.

7. Serve immediately, or warm gently before serving.

Protein: 11 g

Dark Chocolate Peanut Butter Cocoa

Hope Comerford, Clinton Township, MI

Makes 10–12 servings

Prep Time: 5 minutes   Cook Time: 5–6 hours   Ideal slow-cooker size: 3- or 4-qt.

8 cups almond milk

½ cup powdered peanut butter

¼ cup turbinado sugar

12 oz. dark chocolate, broken into pieces

1 Tbsp. vanilla extract

1. Combine almond milk, powdered peanut butter, and turbinado sugar in crock.

2. Cover and cook on low for 5 to 6 hours.

3. Stir in chocolate and vanilla until chocolate is melted, then serve.

Protein: 5 g

Recipe & Ingredient Index

Metric Equivalent Measurements

If you're accustomed to using metric measurements, I don't want you to be inconvenienced by the imperial measurements I use in this book.

Use this handy chart, too, to figure out the size of the slow cooker you'll need for each recipe.

Weight (Dry Ingredients)

1 oz		30 g
4 oz	¼ lb	120 g
8 oz	½ lb	240 g
12 oz	¾ lb	360 g
16 oz	1 lb	480 g
32 oz	2 lb	960 g

Slow-Cooker Sizes

1-quart	0.96 l
2-quart	1.92 l
3-quart	2.88 l
4-quart	3.84 l
5-quart	4.80 l
6-quart	5.76 l
7-quart	6.72 l
8-quart	7.68 l

Volume (Liquid Ingredients)

½ tsp.		2 ml
1 tsp.		5 ml
1 Tbsp.	½ fl oz	15 ml
2 Tbsp.	1 fl oz	30 ml
¼ cup	2 fl oz	60 ml
⅓ cup	3 fl oz	80 ml
½ cup	4 fl oz	120 ml
⅔ cup	5 fl oz	160 ml
¾ cup	6 fl oz	180 ml
1 cup	8 fl oz	240 ml
1 pt	16 fl oz	480 ml
1 qt	32 fl oz	960 ml

Length

¼ in	6 mm
½ in	13 mm
¾ in	19 mm
1 in	25 mm
6 in	15 cm
12 in	30 cm

About the Author

Hope Comerford is a mom, wife, elementary music teacher, blogger, recipe developer, public speaker, Young Living Essential Oils essential oil enthusiast/educator, and published author. In 2013, she was diagnosed with a severe gluten intolerance and since then has spent many hours creating easy, practical, and delicious gluten-free recipes that can be enjoyed by both those who are affected by gluten and those who are not.

Growing up, Hope spent many hours in the kitchen with her Meme (her grandmother), and her love for cooking grew from there. While working on her master's degree when her daughter was young, Hope turned to her slow cookers for some salvation and sanity. It was from there she began truly experimenting with recipes and quickly learned she had the ability to get a little more creative in the kitchen and develop her own recipes.

In 2010, Hope started her blog, *A Busy Mom's Slow Cooker Adventures*, to simply share the recipes she was making with her family and friends. She never imagined people all over the world would begin visiting her page and sharing her recipes with others as well. In 2013, Hope self-published her first cookbook, *Slow Cooker Recipes 10 Ingredients or Less and Gluten-Free*, and then later wrote *The Gluten-Free Slow Cooker*.

Hope became the new brand ambassador and author of Fix-It and Forget-It in mid-2016. Since then, she has brought her excitement and creativeness to the Fix-It and Forget-It brand. Through Fix-It and Forget-It, she has written *Fix-It and Forget-It Healthy Slow Cooker Cookbook*, *Fix-It and Forget-It Healthy One-Pot Meals*, *Fix-It and Forget-It Mediterranean Diet Cookbook*, *Fix-It and Forget-It Instant Pot Light & Healthy Cookbook*, *Fix-It and Forget-It Plant-Based Comfort Food Cookbook*, and many more.

Hope lives in the city of Clinton Township, Michigan, near Metro Detroit. She has been happily married to her husband and best friend, Justin, since 2008. Together they have two children, Ella and Gavin, who are her motivation, inspiration, and heart. In her spare time, Hope enjoys traveling, singing, cooking, reading books, working on wooden puzzles, spending time with friends and family, and relaxing.